FROM
MOUNTAINTOP
TO
TABLETOP

FROM
MOUNTAINTOP
TO
TABLETOP

Unlocking the Secrets of Cooking Wild Game

By Matt Pelton

CFI
Springville, UT

ISBN: 1-55517-868-5
v.1

Published by CFI
an imprint of Cedar Fort, Inc.
925 N. Main, Springville, Utah, 84663
www.cedarfort.com

Distributed by:

Cover design by Nicole Williams
Cover design © 2005 by Lyle Mortimer

Printed in the United States of America
10 9 8 7 6 5 4 3 2 1

Printed on acid-free paper

I would like to thank my wife, Katie, and my kids for their patience and understanding, and for allowing me to be who I am. I love you!

CONTENTS

INTRODUCTION

While I was researching the possibility of writing this book, I held some wild game cooking clinics to see what people's reactions would be when I prepared venison for them. Almost 100 percent of the responses were, "I can't believe this is venison," or, "I am going home to cook some venison I have in the freezer."

So many people out there have not learned the art of cooking wild game, and if they only knew how, they would enjoy hunting so much more. I wrote this book to help others understand and learn the art of cooking wild game.

To research this book fully, I have spent the past eight years talking to people across the United States. I have learned their tips and secrets for cooking everything from moose to eastern whitetail, and I have discovered that the process for preparing venison is universal. Yet most people who know it can't explain it. It is something they learned from a father, grandfather, or mother: an art passed from generation to generation.

Today's society relies too much on commercially prepared foods, and as a result, we have lost the art of preparing venison. In this book, I have tried to recapture that art, breaking it down and explaining the process of preparing and cooking venison—from the time you pull the trigger until you serve the meat for dinner. I not only explain how to perform each step but why each step is important. In the final chapters, I have included a sample of my recipes so that you can take what you've read about and put it into practice. Join me in enjoying the art of preparing venison!

The author on a recent moose hunt in Alaska.

MY BEGINNINGS

I began my journey as a hunter at a young age. Starting at the age of five, I followed my dad as he pursued everything from deer to ducks. Hunting was a way of life for most people in Levan, Utah. I don't remember a single boy my age who didn't hunt. We all started out with a Red Rider BB gun, endlessly chasing birds. We were not always successful, but we had fun developing the skills necessary to hunt game.

Even at that young age, we looked forward to the deer hunt every year. Deer camp meant riding horses, camping, and swapping stories around the campfire. However, it meant much more. Deer camp meant a freezer full of the best tasting meat on the planet: venison.

We often depended on Dad's hunting for our meals. We couldn't afford beef as much as we would have liked, so venison showed up on the table. Dad never made it sound like we were poor, however. Instead, he told us that venison was the meat most often served to European royalty! We loved game meat, and we ate it knowing we were eating the finest meat on earth. We didn't even have to be royalty to eat this fine meat; we hunted it right in our own backyard.

I grew up counting down the days until I was old enough to hunt big game. I had hunted with my dad for many years but, in accordance with Utah law, waited until I was fourteen to hunt big game.

A few months after my fourteenth birthday, I shot my first big game animal, a two-point buck mule deer. Opening morning of the season found us hunting some small finger draws above Yuba Reservoir in central Utah. About an hour after first light, we saw a group of four bucks across the canyon four hundred yards away. The lead buck was a four point. I could see his rack clearly as I looked through the scope.

I put the crosshairs of the scope somewhere in the middle of his body and steadied for the shot. I gently pulled back the trigger and jumped—the gun was on safety. My dad grabbed me by the shoulder and said "Not here. Let's hike around to the other ridge and ambush them. We'll be in perfect wind."

I thought my dad was nuts. I knew his plan wouldn't work; besides, I had a four-point in my sights! Nevertheless, I followed him around to the other ridge. It took us twenty minutes to hike over and get set up, and the whole time I was thinking I had lost my chance. Within minutes after we'd set up; however, I heard something coming toward us. A two-point buck was in the lead trotting right at me. My dad whistled, and the buck stopped broadside fifty yards away.

Seeing the buck in front of me, I completely forgot about the four-point buck. I pulled the trigger, and the buck went down straight away. He was still moving a little, so I put another bullet in the chamber and prepared to shoot again. Dad stopped me, saying, "He's not going anywhere, is he?"

Then my training really began. I had never cleaned a deer before, and my dad was not about to do it for me. I shot it, and now I needed to take care of it. I remember how apprehensive I was when I began. My dad was always fast and never seemed to mind cleaning his animals. Why was I so bothered by it?

I made the first cuts, and, seeing that I was not going to come out of this mess with clean hands, I dove in. The warm insides felt great on my hands that were numb with cold that October morning. The sweet smell of deer blood filled my nostrils as I worked through the steam rising all around me. I took a small handful of drift snow and scrubbed the inside, leaving small traces of sagebrush inside. I was lucky; we were able to drive the truck within fifty yards of the deer. My dad left me to drag my deer myself to toughen me up.

When I got home, more work waited. After hosing out the

deer until the carcass was entirely clean, I began to skin the animal—a long process for an unskilled beginner. Finally, we hung the deer in the garage for three days before spending several hours butchering and wrapping the meat. Dad was patient, helping me along the way but never doing it for me. I will never forget the lessons learned doing it myself or the satisfaction I felt every time I cooked and ate my deer. My hunt was not over at the sound of my gunshot. Rather, my life as a hunter had just begun!

Too many times I talk to hunters who shoot a deer, have it butchered, and throw freezer-burned meat to their dogs a year later. How sad to see such fine meat wasted in this way! Most of these hunters eat the meat for the first couple of months then lose interest, or perhaps their family tires of the venison. They are missing out on the total hunting experience; after all, nothing feels more rewarding than feeding your family meat you harvested. Truly, from the mountaintop to the tabletop defines a hunter.

When I met these hunters, I wondered if the outcome would be different if they could taste the venison I prepared. Would they change their mind about eating it then? I began offering to cook their meat and received the same response almost every time. They couldn't believe how good the meat was and could not wait to prepare it the way I taught them.

I genuinely believe that cooking wild game is an art form, one that has been widely lost in this generation. We have life too easy now. My family eats wild game 90 percent of the time. We do not eat it out of necessity, as I did when I was young. I have been blessed with a good job, so we can afford to eat whatever meat we choose. We eat venison because it truly is the best meat out there. Not only is it extremely healthy—full of protein and saturated fats—but it is also rich in flavor and texture. By the time you finish this book, I hope you'll be a venison lover as well.

My dad taught me how to cook venison. I took what he taught me then experimented on my own. I wasn't always successful. In fact, flies have even refused to eat some of my creations! However, over the years, I have learned what does and does not work and have broken it down to a science. There really are some hints and tips that unlock the secrets of venison so that you can enjoy it again and again.

You'll find a lot of recipes at the end of this book. Feel free to try any of them, experimenting and making them your own. I cook in a different manner than most, following principles rather than directions. By reading this book, I hope you can learn and understand the process behind wild game cooking, then incorporate essential principles in your individual cooking style to become your own master chef.

In my quest to become the best chef I can, I have read many wild game cookbooks that amounted to nothing more than a regular cookbooks with a little outdoor flare. *From Mountaintop to Tabletop* is not one of those. This book covers, in detail, the ins and outs of wild game. Whether you are a beginner or a master chef, you'll find something here to learn as you begin your own journey from mountain to tabletop.

I've written this book in a question-and-answer format so you can pick and choose the information that you need. My intent is to offer a logical approach to preparing wild game. My ideas come from years of hunting, eating, and enjoying the experience!

What Is Venison?

Many people think of venison as only deer meat. However, it would be hard to label only deer meat as venison because you'll find so many varieties of deer in the world. It is crazy to suppose that an eastern whitetail tastes like a western mule deer. Venison, then, is defined as any meat belonging to the deer family, including moose, caribou, elk, and all species of deer. Also included in the definition is meat from mountain goats, mountain sheep, and antelope because of similarities in the meat composition.

Lower in fat and cholesterol than most fish, venison is one of the healthiest meats you can eat. The fats in venison are mainly monounsaturated fats that are healthy for you. They are already broken down and are considered instant energy.

To visualize this, picture a bucket full of warm water. Imagine you want to fill the bucket with soapsuds. In one bucket, you use a liquid dish soap like Dawn or Joy. You squirt some in and shake it up. Within a couple of minutes, the dish soap is no longer visible; it has turned to suds.

In another bucket, you place a bar of hand soap, then shake the bucket for five minutes. A few soapsuds appear, but the bar of soap is still visible in the bottom of the bucket. The liquid soap represents the unsaturated fats found in venison, and the bar of soap represents the saturated fats found in most domestic meats. Whether you realize it, fats are essential for your body to survive. The basic difference is that unsaturated fats go to work right away while saturated fats require a lot to break them down into usable elements. Saturated fats also stimulate the production of LDL cholesterol, which can clog arteries.

Venison is also high in proteins, which are essential to your survival as well. Composed of entirely red muscle tissue, venison contains more protein than white muscle tissue does, which makes up most domestic meats. Thanks to the rich, natural forage that members of the deer family eat, venison is full of essential vitamins and minerals, and you don't have to worry about growth hormones or other harmful chemicals. Wild animals that have clean feed and clean air rarely get sick; the ones that do usually end up as the victims of predators such as mountain lions and coyotes. Venison ranges in flavor from robust western mule deer that feed mainly on sagebrush to sweet, mild eastern whitetail deer that feed on acorns and clovers. Venison is a perfect meat source.

In summary, regardless of the species, all venison share similar traits, including:

• Low in saturated fats—less than 1 percent.

• Higher in monounsaturated fats—the healthy type of fat (still less than three grams per serving).

• High in proteins and essential amino acids—essential for muscle development.

• Free of chemicals and artificial growth hormones.

• Low in harmful bacteria.

• Tender, flavorful meat.

• A good source of Omega 3 fatty acids—essential for brain development and well-being.

The Nature of Blood

The morning of my first deer hunt, I looked at the deer lying on the ground in front of me. *What do I do now?* I wondered. I had seen my dad harvest several deer, but I realized I hadn't paid a lot of attention.

"Slit his throat and bleed him out," my dad instructed.

Oh, yeah. Now I remembered. I grabbed my pocketknife and started sawing away at the windpipe halfway up the throat. "No, cut into it and pull the knife out," Dad said. I did as I was told, but nothing came out. "Did you cut the jugulars?" my dad asked.

"I don't know," I replied. I cut a little deeper, and a small trickle of blood appeared. My dad helped me turn the head downhill, and I massaged the rib cage with my foot. After all was said and done, maybe a pint of blood was the ground. I wondered what happened to all the rest of the blood.

My question was answered as soon as we cut into the carcass. I had hit both lungs and part of the heart, and most of the blood was inside the carcass. The main reason for bad taste in wild game meat is the presence of blood. Blood by its very nature is unstable. It has to be to keep us alive. Red blood cells absorb oxygen from our lungs then transfer it throughout our bodies where it is absorbed into muscles and burned into energy. It is because of this principle that blood taints the flavor of wild game.

Why does blood taint the meat?

When blood is exposed to outside air, it breaks down rapidly and begins to decompose. If any blood is left in the meat, muscle fibers begin to absorb the tainted blood as it would absorb oxygen, leaving that flavor behind. In addition, any outside elements that come in contact with blood transfer their flavor to the meat. If meat is exposed to dirt and fuel in your truck, the meat absorbs those flavors. Game flavor is often compared to liver flavor. This makes sense because liver is made up of 80 percent blood.

Most hunters, and even many nonhunters, have heard that if you shoot a running animal the meat is inedible. That's because the muscles are engorged with blood at the time of the kill, and if it is not removed, the blood taints the meat. When you exercise, your body uses energy and requires extra oxygen. Consequently, all the blood vessels in your body open and fill with blood. Maybe you've noticed that after a workout your hands are swollen and tight when you squeeze them. This is a sign that the vessels in your hands are full of blood.

The same thing happens with animals. At rest, blood flow is at a minimum. However, when an animal runs, its muscles fill with blood. If you shoot a running animal and don't care for the meat properly, the meat truly tastes terrible! On the flip side, an animal that is shot as it is preparing to sleep or just waking up almost always tastes wonderful. So do you pass up the chance to shoot a running buck? No, you simply need to know how to care for the meat, and you can enjoy great-tasting venison every time.

How long does it take for blood to taint the meat?

In the hot summer months and into the early fall, meat can become tainted in only a few minutes. In the winter months, you have several hours before damage is done. The main objective during this time is to get as much blood out of the animal as possible.

How do I properly bleed out an animal?

The easiest way is to slit the throat. Ideally, you should turn the animal with its head angled downhill. Insert your knife halfway up the neck, about two inches in from the windpipe; keep the blade parallel to the windpipe and make sure the knife cuts completely through and is exposed underneath. Then turn the blade and saw out, cutting completely through the windpipe.

If you do this correctly, some blood should drain out immediately. If no blood appears, make sure that you've cut the jugular veins all the way through. If not, repeat the process, cutting back a little further.

Once blood spills out, massage the chest region of the animal as if you're doing CPR. Remember: the more blood you get out, the better.

How do I bleed out an animal that I plan to cape out for a mount?

In this instance, position the rear quarters of the animal downhill. Lift the top leg up and slice towards the hip in the pocket between the leg and groin area. Cut in until you find the femoral artery along the large bone of the leg. Do the same to the other leg. Position the animal on its back with the rear legs apart and massage the blood out.

The femoral artery is larger than the jugular and, in my opinion, is a more effective way to bleed out an animal. Unfortunately, most hunters choose not to bleed out when they harvest a quality animal. If they do bleed the animal out, they wait until they have removed the cape. However, remember the cardinal rule: the faster you can get the blood out of an animal, the better.

How do I bleed out an animal that was shot while running?

Few things are more difficult than this. However, every hunter at one time or another shoots an animal on the run. Don't despair—all hope for good venison is not lost. First, cut both the jugular and femoral arteries as quickly as possible. Massage the chest cavity vigorously. Immediately start cleaning the animal.

As soon as the animal is cleaned, begin skinning it. This

cools down the carcass and constricts the blood vessels that are engorged with blood. The quicker you cool down the carcass, the better chance you have of obtaining good-tasting venison. If there is a running stream nearby, quarter the animal. Then wash off the quarters by immersing them in the water and scrubbing them in the stream. Let them sit for a few minutes to drop the temperature and expel the blood. Whether or not it is safe to wash off your meat in stream water has been the subject of much debate. Personally, I see nothing wrong with it. Of course, I don't wash off a carcass in standing water. Mountain streams, however, are generally between forty and forty-eight degrees. Heat transfer only occurs in one direction, so as heat leaves an object, the object cools down. When you wash off a carcass in a stream, the heat from the meat attempts to regulate the temperature of the running water. The water, of course, never heats up; the meat is cooled, and the remaining blood is washed away. There are other advantages to this as well. In addition to washing away the blood, you've washed away gastric juices and urine that may have tainted the meat during the cleaning process.

Some people say that water-born bacteria infects the meat when you do this, and that wet meat spoils faster. The amount of bacteria in a swift mountain stream is minimal. In fact, the most prevalent harmful bacteria found in water is giardia, sometimes called beaver fever. Giardia can only survive in water, so as soon as the meat dries off, the giardia die.

A far greater danger comes from E coli, which exists in animal feces. Anytime feces, or even a cut intestine, touches meat, the meat can become infected with this life-threatening bug. Washing off meat in a stream washes away the feces and any other E coli carrier. Frankly, there is no way to guarantee that you rid your meat of all bacteria; all you can do is try and minimize it.

The theory that meat spoils faster when wet is absurd. As I mentioned, heat can only transfer in one direction, and heat is what spoils meat. So which would spoil quicker, ninety-degree meat or meat cooled to fifty degrees? To put it simply: cooling the meat quickly is the best thing that you can do.

CLEANING YOUR GAME

On my first hunt, I brought along a huge sheath knife just like the one I saw on *Rambo*. I took it out of its sheath to begin cleaning out my deer. "What in the hell are you going to do with that thing?" my dad asked. "Put that ugly thing away and pull out your pocketknife."

I had an Old Timer two-blade in my pocket. I loved knives, and this one was razor sharp. I struggled to keep down my breakfast as I cut around the anus and tied it off. When it came to removing the genitals, I was all right; I had castrated many animals growing up doing ranch work. I finished cleaning the deer in about fifteen minutes. I wiped the excess blood from the carcass with snow. I tried to wash my arms off as well, to no avail. The blood had already dried, as had the spots on my clothes. But it wasn't as bad as I thought it would be, and I was grateful my dad had me do it. Now I could do it on my own.

Cleaning out your animal is a skill most often learned by watching someone: a father, brother, uncle, or other experienced hunter. There's not necessarily a wrong or right way. The object is simply to remove the unwanted portions—stomach, intestines, kidneys, bladder, lungs, and reproductive organ—of the game. These parts of the animal are generally considered unfit in our culture, and they make a nice meal for a scavenger. On the other hand, many prize the heart and liver as prized table fare.

If you can't learn how to clean out your game by watching someone, the process I describe here should suffice and is the fastest, cleanest way I know.

What tools do I need?

Honestly, the only tool you need is a small pocketknife. Too many people do what I did and drag along large sheath knifes into the field. The only purpose I have found for a large sheath knife is to crack the sternum of a carcass. I have rarely needed to do this, however, so I eliminate the extra weight and bulk and leave it at home.

Make sure your knife is as sharp as possible. If you don't know how to sharpen it, it's worth purchasing a high-end knife, such as Spyderco or Lone Wolfe, which doesn't require the same upkeep on the edge. I personally carry an Old Timer two-blade which I've carried for a number of years.

I also carry field-dressing gloves, which I buy at Wal-Mart for a dollar. These handy kits contain a pair of shoulder-length plastic gloves, a pair of Latex exam gloves, and two rubber bands. If you don't want to buy a kit, you can put your own together quickly and easily. They're worth the time and effort. I find them extremely helpful in keeping myself clean when I clean an animal. Gone are the days where I thought being up to my neck in blood was macho!

The only other items I carry with me are a few small zip ties. I use these to attach hunting tags and also to close off the anus to prevent feces from contacting the meat.

Where do I start?

First, cut around the anus and pull it out a few inches. Take a zip tie and cinch it tight around the anus to prevent any feces from touching the meat. Second, cut around the genitals and carefully remove them; do this whether the animal is male or female. In certain areas, law requires that proof of sex is left attached to the carcass. When this is the case, cut around the scrotum and remove the penis, then leave the scrotum with at least one testicle attached to the hindquarter. If it is female, leave the vulva attached to the leg.

After you've removed the genitals, make an incision along the center line of the belly stretching from the genitals to the sternum (chest bone). Cut lightly until the skin and the stomach muscles are separated. Take care not to cut too deep. If you do, you'll know! Green fluid seeps out, and you'll smell a strong odor. If this happens, don't despair, just be careful not to dump out the rumen content.

Once the gut cavity is open and exposed, turn the animal on its side. Most of the intestines and stomach should fall out. There is no fun or easy way to do this. Reach into the gut cavity and rake the guts out. Take special care with the bladder; it bursts easily. Reach into the carcass and cut away the lungs and heart, then cut the windpipe as high up as you can reach it. The liver should be light purple to maroon and slightly triangular. If it has dark spots, it will be inedible.

You can never be too thorough when cleaning an animal. The more you do at this critical stage, the better your meat will taste. Don't expect to do this in fifteen minutes or less at first. However, the more you do it, the faster you will become; the faster you clean an animal, the quicker the meat cools down; the quicker the meat cools down, the better it will taste. I can clean a deer completely in about ten minutes, but I have been doing it for years.

Cooling your meat is absolutely essential in creating a quality end product. Any way that you can accomplish this is helpful. As I mentioned before, if you have a running stream nearby, use it. Nothing cools down a carcass quicker than running water. The first thing a slaughterhouse does after removing the guts is to spray the gut cavity out with water. Not only does it clean the carcass, it cools it down quickly. Snow works great to clean out the cavity as well. If there is snow on the ground, I gather as much as I can and fill the gut cavity. I then make snowballs with the snow inside, vigorously scrubbing the inside with the snowball, then discarding it.

How do I cool meat that I harvest in warm weather?

Because most archery hunts in the west begin in mid-to-late August when daytime temperatures can reach the midnineties, most bow hunters face this challenge. I take these few extra precautions:

- It is absolutely essential that you clean and bleed out an animal as soon as you can. Draining the blood shouldn't be too much of a problem. An arrow kills by cutting through veins and arteries, causing the animal to bleed to death.

- Skin and quarter the animal as soon as possible. Even if it is only a deer or an antelope, skinning and quartering it cools down the meat quickly. If there is a stream nearby, soak the animal in the stream for an hour or so.

- I carry old pillowcases to keep the quarters in. This keeps the meat cool and protects it against wasps and flies. Another trick I use is to bring along rolls of cheesecloth or muslin fabric. I soak it in water, then wrap the meat in "mummy" style. I also carry a canister of aerosol computer cleaner. These cleaners use nitrogen, an inert gas. If you turn the canister upside down, it emits liquid nitrogen. The liquid nitrogen flash freezes the mummy wrap and keeps it cool for a number of hours. I only need one canister for a deer or antelope and two for an elk or moose.

- Keep your animal out of direct sunlight. If at all possible, drag your animal into the shade. Sunlight is your worst enemy. If you have to travel in the sun, cover your meat as much as possible. I often drape my jackets over meat to help insulate it against the sunlight. Most people think that the extra fabric will warm the meat, but this is not the case. Remember that heat only travels one direction. The extra layers insulate against the sunlight, leaving the meat cool. It sounds crazy, but it is science, so heavily insulate your chilled meat to keep it from warming up.

- Make haste in getting your meat off the mountain. The

quicker you can get the meat to a meat locker or home in your fridge, the better. Call ahead of time to meat or cold-storage lockers; many of them store meat for a reasonable rate. If you do a lot of warm-weather hunting, look for a used freezer to cool and store your meat. This will be an invaluable investment if you are a serious hunter. Many thrift stores have them for under one hundred dollars, which is less than what you may pay a meat cutter. When I hunt during warm weather, I keep several coolers full of ice in my truck or in camp. If I have a long drive home, I stop at the first gas station or grocery store and pack my meat in ice. If you take the necessary precautions, you won't have any trouble obtaining quality meat, even during an early-season hunt.

Of course, if you hunt late seasons, you won't have to worry about this. I remember a late season doe hunt my dad and I went on in December. The only way I can describe the hunt is to say it was like shooting fish in a barrel. During Utah winters, the mountain valleys and foothills are lousy with deer. The high terrain they inhabit most of the year is sometimes covered with ten feet of snow, and they have to head downhill. If you are lucky enough to draw a late season doe hunt, you are almost assured success.

This was definitely the case with this hunt. By 9 A.M., we had the deer tagged and loaded into the truck. The temperature was in the neighborhood of twenty degrees. By the time we stopped to fuel up, the deer were frozen solid. To this day, that was some of the best venison I have ever tasted.

The steps of cleaning and cooling the meat is probably the least understood and most important in harvesting quality meat. Follow these steps, and if you do, I promise you you'll have better meat every time.

Here is a list of the most common mistakes when cleaning out game:
- Leaving the anus in the carcass
- Breaking the bladder

- Cutting open the rumen
- Leaving the heart and lungs in the carcass
- Leaving the windpipe in the carcass
- Leaving the kidneys in the carcass
- Not washing out the gut cavity as soon as possible
- Leaving feces in the carcass
- Leaving the genitals intact

When you harvest a late-season animal, the meat almost always tastes better because it cools quickly. Photo courtesy of Randy Judd

Packing Them Out

On my first deer hunt, I was lucky—or so I thought. "Start dragging the deer," he said, as he hiked back to the truck. The dirt road was a hundred yards away, so we drove the truck off the road to the brink of the hill. That way I only had to go fifty yards with the deer.

That won't be so bad, I thought. *How could it be? It's only a deer, and I only have to go a fifty yards. No problem.* At the time, I stood about five foot nine and weighed about one hundred and twenty pounds. Not knowing a lot about physics, I didn't understand the struggle I would have dragging one hundred and seventy five pounds of dead weight uphill.

I grabbed the deer by its horn and gave it a pull. At first, all I did was stretch the animal out. After I counted to three, I lunged, moving the carcass a couple of feet. I tried again with a similar result. By this time, I was breathing hard and looking for possible routes my dad could use to drive the old Ford down the hill to my deer. After another five minutes, I looked back, exhausted. I couldn't believe my eyes! I was less than twenty yards from the gut pile. My arm was getting numb. *I don't remember the hill being this steep when I shot this animal,* I thought.

I could imagine my dad laughing as he watched my feeble attempts, but I knew he would be proud as could be, seeing me accomplishing it. I wanted to show him I could do it. *I shot it, and by hell, I'll drag it out,* I silently vowed. By the time the truck pulled into view, I was ready to collapse. I had dragged that deer within ten yards of the road. My dad helped me drag it the rest of the way and throw it into the truck. That's when I learned a valuable lesson about hunting: the work begins *after* the trigger is pulled.

No doubt you've been in a similar situation. Some pack-outs may be as simple as loading the animal onto a four-wheeler and driving it out. Others may require you to bone out a seven-hundred pound elk and haul it out in backpacks because you couldn't even take a horse where you shot your elk. Whatever the case, it is always work.

We would all like to see that big bull fall just off the road or four-wheeler trail. How would that be? Unfortunately, 90 percent of the time, that doesn't happen. In fact, the "big boys" will be as far away as possible to try to avoid meeting up with you and your 180-grain, lead-cored, copper-jacketed friend. You can't expect your prey to relocate for your convenience.

So what do you do? Leave him? Of course not! You are a hunter, and he is the reason you are here. Once on a spike elk hunt in Utah with my wife's uncle, we went to a high saddle where he had seen elk pass through. After a three-hour hike and fifteen hundred vertical feet through tangles of rose hips, vine maples, and aspen suckers, I began to reconsider my desire to kill an elk—at least here. I kept wondering how we would get an elk out. The trail was too steep for a horse, and it was not a hike that I wanted to take more than once in a single day. However, if the opportunity arose to harvest a Boone and Crockett bull, I knew I would take it, regardless of the work. A spike bull, on the other hand, wasn't nearly as appealing in this situation.

This is a decision you have to make the deeper you head into the hunting grounds. If you kill an animal, you have the legal and ethical responsibility to pack it out. Anything less is pure cowardice, and anybody who leaves a magnificent creature where he killed it will get their due in the end.

How do I pack an animal out?

Nowadays most people use four-wheelers to haul out their game. These machines have changed the entire profile of our sport. They are tough and relatively inexpensive to operate. In a lot of western states, four-wheeler trails are everywhere. And where trails exist, four-wheelers are very useful in packing out game.

I have a problem with this method, however, when people leave designated trails and start tearing up the forest habitat with them. I do not condone this, and I hope none of you fit in that category! Because of this, four-wheelers are banned in many state and federal land areas.

If you do use a four-wheeler, be aware of weight restrictions and balance. Every year, sportsmen are killed or crippled because their vehicles were either overloaded or off balance. If you follow the safety precautions and take the time to secure a balanced load, there isn't a more effective way to haul out big game.

I like hunting in the backcountry where four-wheelers aren't allowed. For my type of hunting, nothing works better than a horse. Horses can carry several hundred pounds of meat through rugged terrain. There are many ways to pack out meat on a horse. If you have a packsaddle with panniers, that is the best way. Simply load the quarters in the panniers, making sure to load one rear and one front per pannier to even the load. The back straps and loose meat can be distributed over the whole frame. The antlers and cape can be lashed to the sawbuck frame with the head or skull plate in front of the buck with the antlers sweeping back towards the rear.

If you don't have a packsaddle, you can use a regular riding saddle in much the same way. After the animal is quartered, put the quarters in heavy-duty game bags; cheesecloth will not work. I use heavy canvas or at least king-size pillowcases. Do not use plastic under any circumstances. Meat needs to breathe to remain fresh. After you've sealed the meat up in game bags, lash the quarters together at the lower joint and drape them over the saddle. Use twine or duct tape to secure the quarters to the saddle horn and cantle of the saddle. When the meat is secure, walk the horse off the mountain.

If you don't own or have access to a horse, other options are available. The most common method for hauling out meat in the western states is a backpack or a meat frame. You'll need two items for either of these: twine or duct tape, and heavy-game bags.

First, quarter out the animal and secure the meat into the game bags. Whether you use a backpack or a meat frame, you can usually take only one-quarter at a time of a moose, elk, or large deer. If you need to make additional trips, hang the remaining quarters high off the ground to prevent spoiling and contamination. In most states, you are not allowed to take out the antlers and cape until the meat is hauled out. Be aware of your state regulations and act accordingly.

Use the twine to secure the quarter to your backpack, using the frame and the rings of the pack. Pick up the pack and test it to make sure the load is secure. An insecure or unbalanced load is actually dangerous. Your body will strain to support the weight. A good friend of mine actually rolled down a steep hill and broke his ankle because of an unbalanced load.

A meat frame has the nice feature of a built-in shelf to secure the bulk of the weight. When you have the meat secure and are ready to pack it out, set the backpack upright and sit down to slip it on. This prevents back injury that may occur when you're swinging a lot of weight onto your back. You may find situations where it is dangerous to carry out a full quarter of whatever animal you've shot. If so, bone out all the meat and secure it in game bags in portions that you can carry out, given the terrain. You'll be much better off taking a couple of extra trips rather than risking serious injury.

In my experience, deer can usually be dragged out, rather than quartered. A roll of clothesline, a piece of foam pad, and duct tape are invaluable pulling tools. Wrap the clothesline around the animal's body and then around the neck near the jawbone. Fashion a handle around a loop of the clothesline with the foam pad and duct tape. This approach relieves a significant amount of strain from dragging your animal, plus it makes it easier for two or more people to drag the carcass out.

You'll find many products available today aimed at making animal removal easier and quicker. These include wheeled carts, sleds, and a travois system. These are all very effective but are limited to the terrain you find yourself in. If you are hunting in relatively mild terrain, you'll find these products useful; they can even save time and prevent damage to your game. However, in much of the rough, precipitous terrain of the west, these products are impractical and even dangerous. These products can range from under fifty dollars to several hundred dollars. Let you budget be your guide. Don't apply for a second mortgage just to get your hands on one of these. They may not make that much difference!

How do I quarter out a big-game animal?

Begin by laying the animal on its side. Skin the animal from the legs to the middle of the back; the whole side of the animal should be exposed. Start with the front quarter, lift up the leg, and in a sweeping motion, cut away the connective tissue underneath while lifting. Continue doing this until the quarter separates from the carcass. When it is free, secure the quarter in a game bag and set it aside.

To remove the rear quarter, lift it up as you did the front. Make a cut underneath and towards the hip or ball-and-socket joint to free the joint. Cut around and into the joint until it breaks free. When the joint is free, cut around the muscle groups, removing the connective tissue until the quarter is free. Leave as much meat on the quarter as possible. When the quarter is free, secure it into a game bag and set it aside.

Remove the back strap by making a horizontal incision along the ribs three-quarters of the way up the ribs. Peel up on the meat while you cut along the ribs and into the vertebrae pocket until the back strap is free. Turn the carcass over and repeat the process.

When the quarters and back straps are free, remove the tenderloins, which are located on the inside of the rib cage along the vertebrae. Remove them, as you did the back straps, by peeling the meat while cutting along the bones. I like to carry the back straps, tenderloins, heart, and liver in the same bag.

The first few times you skin a deer or elk this way will take a while. After you have done it several times; however, it becomes easier and faster. I can generally completely quarter an elk in thirty to forty-five minutes.

In packing out meat, remember there's no right or wrong way. Keep the meat clean and cool, and spend as little time as possible packing it out. Whether you have horses, four-wheelers, or backpacks, hauling out your meat will take work. Remember: the real work of hunting begins after the animal is down.

Sometimes, even with a large animal like this moose, you can only haul the meat out with a backpack.

AGING MEAT

I hung up my first deer from the rafters in our tool shed. I used an old broomstick handle, and I inserted it between the large tendons at the hock and the bone. We used a come-along to lift the carcass up into the rafters. I cut the head off at the neck with a large meat saw that resembled a large hacksaw. We inserted a 2 x 4 in the rib cage to open the carcass up. We let the carcass hang for three days before we cut it up. I didn't know what I was doing or why I was doing it. I only knew that this is what my dad did with deer, and what my grandpa had done with deer before that.

So, what benefits *do* come from aging meat? And how do you age meat properly? Why bother? People often ask me these questions; let's look at the answers.

I use meat-aging techniques with almost every animal I kill, although it's not always necessary with wild game. In fact, when working in hot weather, sometimes it is much better to simply cool and cut your meat. However, when conditions are right, aging techniques tenderize your meat and mellow the flavor.

What is aging meat?

The process of aging or curing meat simply means shrinking the muscle fibers to tenderize the meat. To understand this, it helps to understand how muscle groups are put together. If you pull apart an orange and break open a slice, you will notice hundreds of strands of juice-filled pockets.

Muscle fibers are structured in a similar manner. Thousands of strands of muscles are bound together by tendons at the ends, connecting them to bone. Small protein "hairs" also bind them together individually. When the meat shrinks, these hairs pull apart and break, resulting in more tender meat. Bacteria also help break the meat down, adding more tenderness.

Understanding how meat is graded also can help you understand the importance of aging it. Muscles become larger when bundles of muscles are stressed and the fibers pull apart, allowing individual fibers to become larger in diameter. The diameter of individual muscle fibers is referred to in the meat industry as the quality grade. The larger the muscle fiber, the poorer quality grade the meat is. The United States Department of Agriculture (USDA) grades meat in the following categories, from highest quality to lowest: prime, choice, select, and utility.

- USDA utility grade meat generally comes from older animals, especially bull cattle and milking cows. Utility grade meat is used for hot dogs, sausage, and potted meats.

- USDA select grade meat is the most common meat available. Most grocery stores stock select grade beef.

- USDA choice grade meat is the best meat available for the public market place. Grocery stores that carry USDA choice proudly advertise that fact, as well they should. Choice grade is far superior meat to select grade beef.

- USDA prime meat is usually only found in specialty meat shops or high-quality restaurants. It is the highest quality meat available and is the most tender and moist.

The other meat grading system is yield grade, or the percentage of saturated fat in meat. Most beef yields 5–8 percent, meaning the meat contains 5–8 percent saturated fat. Twenty years ago, most beef yielded 10–15 percent because the public generally wanted more fat in beef because it had more flavor and was more tender. Beef producers today, however, have listened to consumer demand to produce a lower fat, higher quality beef.

An average elk steak graded on these systems would earn a quality grade of prime and a yield grade below 1 percent. Venison is simply the healthiest meat you can eat—higher in meat quality than any other meat source. The public is becoming aware of this, and a number of elk ranches are popping up across the country to meet this demand.

How long do I age my meat?

Most of you have eaten at restaurants that advertise beef that has been aged twenty-four days. Why? Generally speaking, the longer you age meat, the more tender it becomes. Of course, the process varies a bit. What we are trying to do is shrink the meat 10 percent to achieve maximum tenderness. The process generally takes longer in a larger animal, such as a moose or a larger elk; an antelope or deer takes less time. However, twenty-four days seems to be the ideal threshold. Meat aged longer than this often actually becomes dry instead of aged.

You also have to determine beforehand if the meat actually needs to be aged. Properly aged beef will have a bite pressure rating of five to eight pounds of pressure per bite. A freshly killed antelope rates only three to five pounds of pressure per bite. The bite rating system was developed to rate the tenderness of meat. It refers to the pressure needed to bite through a piece of meat. If aged to full capacity, antelope only rates one to two pounds per bite, or approximately the same texture as liver. Freshly killed deer and elk rate between five and seven pounds per bite. This rating, of course, is affected by the age and condition of the animal. I always age an older animal longer than a younger one because the older animals have more protein strands binding the meat together.

I always recommend aging meat at least one day if the conditions are good. Aging also allows the meat to relax and expel any extra blood that may have been left behind. That excess blood causes what people call "game" flavor in meat.

How do I age my meat?

To age your meat, hang the carcass in a cool, dry place with plenty of air and no direct sunlight. Direct sunlight causes age spots that produce bacteria. Age meat in temperatures between thirty-five and forty-eight degrees. This is cool enough that bacteria will not infect the meat but warm enough that the meat will shrink. As the moisture leaves the meat, the muscle fibers pull apart, breaking protein stands and tenderizing the meat.

Most people hang the carcass in a shed or a garage. Even if the temperature outside is between fifty and sixty degrees, a garage or shed stays cool enough during the day to keep the meat from spoiling. Leave the door closed so warm temperatures outside don't heat the inside. If outside temperatures reach above sixty-five degrees, butcher the meat immediately or store it in the refrigerator.

If you can, split the carcass in half. If you can't, at least insert a board between the ribs to open the carcass. Of course, if your meat is quartered, this step is unnecessary.

I have heard many people debate the issue of aging with skin on or off. Some people argue that leaving the skin on protects the meat from insects and bacteria while still allowing the meat to cure. A number of studies have been done on this subject, and nothing could be further than the truth. Extensive research was done on the question of curing antelope at the University of Wyoming. Though researchers found no difference in the end result as far as bite rating and tenderness, the difference in bacteria present was unnerving. Meat cured with skin still on had four thousand times the amount of bacteria!

Why? The skin is a powerful insulator, and it creates hot spots between the meat and the skin where life flourishes. I never recommend aging meat with the skin on. If you are worried about insects, age your meat in breathable game bags, but keep in mind that when meat is air dried, the outside layer forms a shield that keeps out bacteria. The meat inside will be as fresh as the day it was harvested. This outside dried layer can be easily cut off and discarded; I save it for dog snacks.

When I age my meat, I measure the circumference of the largest portion of the hindquarter. I remeasure every day until there is a 10 percent loss in the girth, usually three to five days for a deer and twelve to fifteen days for a large elk or moose. A bison may take the full twenty-four days before reaching the ideal 10 percent mark.

Take care when you hang your meat. Make sure it isn't touching anything. If the meat contacts any surface, such as a nearby wall, heat from that surface may transfer into the meat, causing a hot spot. These spots produce extra bacteria and cause the meat to spoil. On the other hand, if meat contacts a cold concrete floor, heat from the meat transfers to the floor, leaving the meat too cold to age properly.

Can I cure meat killed in the warm weather?

Hunters ask me this question all the time. Certainly, since aging meat tenderizes it and adds flavor, aging meat is desirable year-round.

The best option is to locate a meat locker or cold-storage unit that offers hanging rates. Call ahead and reserve a space; they tend to fill up quickly during hunting season. If you cannot find one, you can use an old fridge. I've found one at a second-hand store for around a hundred bucks. If you hunt as much as I do, that hundred dollars is money well spent. Cold storage can cost you half that much to hang one animal.

If you opt for the fridge, remove all the shelves, and build a rack that you can hang the meat from. If you need to cure an elk or a large deer, you may need to bone out the meat and lay it on racks to cure.

Sometimes, the best option is simply to cool down the meat, package it, and freeze it, depending on the situation and your desire for the meat. Most antelope, deer, and elk are tender enough that during the summer months I simply cool them, cut them, and freeze them.

The process of aging meat is probably the least understood but the most beneficial in regards to enjoying tender meat. Remember these tips:

- Skin the meat! I cannot stress this enough for health reasons.
- Hang the meat in a cool, dry place, such as a garage, shed, or meat locker.
- Make sure the temperature of the meat doesn't rise above fifty degrees.
- Do not let the meat touch anything.
- Make sure the meat does not come in contact with direct light.
- Split the carcass in half or spread the rib cage.
- In warm months, it is better not to age the meat if circumstances don't allow you to follow these steps.

Follow these time recommendations:
- Antelope: one to three days
- Deer: three to five days
- Elk: seven to ten days
- Large elk and moose: twelve to fifteen days
- Bison: fourteen to twenty-four days

If you like to be exact, measure so you know when your meat loses the ideal 10 percent in girth.

Cutting and Packaging Meat

Three days after I killed my first deer, I came home to find the kitchen table covered with paper, as well as an assortment of knives, bowls, and cutting boards. My dad was home from work and ready to help me to butcher my deer. I had helped my dad butcher deer and elk since I was old enough to walk, but this time was different.

"What do you want to do with your deer?" he asked. I didn't know I had a choice. At the time, my favorite thing in the world was homemade jerky, so that was an instant request. I also loved bottled-meat sandwiches, so bottled meat was a must. Deer steaks were and still are one of my favorite things to eat, so I asked for those. My family had a tradition of always eating the tenderloins when we finished butchering the deer, so that too came to mind.

Dad and I sat down and made a list, starting with the front quarters and working our way to the back straps. I learned the difference between a steak and a fillet. I also learned what cuts were used for which type of meat product. I had seen my dad do this many times, but I never paid close attention before.

That year, I mixed my first batch of marinade for jerky and started soaking it. Every time I ate meat from my deer, I felt a sense of pride and accomplishment because I had done it all, from shooting and hauling to aging and butchering.

How do I start cutting?

The first and most important step is to make a list of what you want. A typical list might look like this:

- Roasts
- Steaks
- Bottled meat
- Jerky
- Ground meat
- Scraps (dog food)

Start your list while your animal is hanging so you will be prepared when you are ready to cut it. Discuss requests with your family. List what you want in the order you want it. For example, I like to have more meat cut into steaks than ground meat. However, families that eat a lot of dishes with ground beef should list ground meat as their number one item. Families that don't care much for wild game but love jerky should jerk most of the meat.

Make choices that are ethical and use up your meat. I hate to see the amount of venison that is thrown out every year because people don't plan ahead for what they want. Even if you decide that you don't want to cut up your own game, make a list to give to your butcher so he can accommodate your desires.

What tools do I need?

A lot of people don't cut up their own game because they don't think that they have the right tools. However, most people have the necessary tools right in their kitchen. The basics include:

- Meat cleaver
- Boning knife
- Fillet knife (not essential but helpful)
- Cutting boards
- Large bowls
- Knife-sharpening device
- Plastic bags (gallon size, freezer variety)
- Plastic wrap or vacuum packer

- Butcher paper (waxed)
- Masking tape
- Large table or working area
- Permanent black marker

In my home, we set up tables in the kitchen and establish a bit of an assembly line. I bone out (cut the meat away from the bones) the game and cut the pieces identified on the list. My kids place the pieces in the appropriate bowls. My wife wraps up and packages the meat. It takes us about two hours to cut up a deer and three to four hours to cut up an elk.

How do I know where to begin and how to cut?

I start by cutting up the front quarters, which are the most difficult and time consuming. I do these first because if I save them for the last, I am bound to get lazy and not do the best job.

The actual process of cutting the meat is simple. First, separate the carcass into quarters. Cut off the purple, dried, outside layer of meat, but save it. This makes excellent and healthy dog snacks. Remove all the meat from the bones; keep as much of the meat as possible intact. Cut the meat up into roasts, steaks, and other cuts you want.

After you have removed the purple skin from the front quarter, remove the meat from the bone by locating the ridge in the shoulder blade. This ridge runs from the top to the bottom of the front quarter on the outside. Cut down along this bone, peeling back the meat as you go. Repeat the process on the other side of the bone. Continue peeling the meat off the bone until it is free. Set the bones aside or discard them. After removing all the bones, remove any visible silver tissue and chunks of fat. These contain the unsaturated fats, which taste strongly of whatever the animal had been eating.

Understanding the different cuts of meat and where they are found on the animal is critical. A roast is any cut of meat larger than one pound. Roasts can be cut as a fillet or a steak. Pot roast

FROM MOUNTAINTOP TO TABLETOP

and London broils are steaks larger than one pound. Round roasts and rib roasts are fillets larger than one pound.

A steak is a cut of meat crosscut with the grain. A properly cut steak has the grain running almost straight up and down. As a general rule, any steak cut more than three inches thick is considered a roast. Some common steaks cut from wild game are:

- Loin steaks
- Shoulder steaks
- Sirloin steaks
- Round steaks
- Filet mignons (tenderloin steaks)

A fillet is a cut of meat cut along the grain. Most of the time, filet mignon is mislabeled and is prepared as a steak with the grain running up and down. The cut received its name because a true filet mignon will be thicker than it is in diameter, making it a fillet. Some of the most common fillets cut from wild game are:

- Round roasts
- Shank roasts
- Rib roasts
- Whole or half tenderloins

All of the meat used for jerky, bottled meat, and ground meat is cut from what is left after you have cut your roasts and steaks.

You can't get many steaks or roasts from the front quarters of a deer. I usually cut most of the front quarters into jerky and bottled meat. I never cut up venison for stew meat. It doesn't last long in a freezer and is difficult to cook with good results. (See the cooking section for a more complete discussion.)

However, if you are cutting up a large deer, elk, or moose, the front quarter has the potential of some nice chuck steaks and roasts. For steaks, separate the muscle groups out and cut the steaks across the grain three-quarters of an inch to an inch thick. This may require that you cut slightly diagonally to get steaks that have the grain running straight up and down. The straighter you can get the grains, the easier to prepare and more tender the meat will be.

For chuck roasts, don't separate the muscle groups. Instead, cut them as large, thick crosscuts at least three inches thick. When you cut meat for jerky, cut it into a thin fillet with the grain one-eighth inch thick.

Any meat you plan to bottle or grind doesn't have to be cut in any particular way, but it will be easier to process if the chunks are less than two inches square. I, personally, cut all available meat into roasts because roasts last longer in the freezer. Plus, if freezer burn occurs, you can always cut off the portion of freezer-burned roast and still use the remainder. If you have freezer burn on steaks, however, you almost always have to throw the steaks out. If I want steaks, I thaw out a roast and cut it into steaks. I do the same thing if I want stew meat—thaw out a roast and cut stew meat.

After you cut the quarter into the cuts you want, separate them into large bowls on your work area. I have one bowl for steaks and roasts, one for jerky strips, one for small meat chunks to bottle and grind, and one for scraps. This system works well, especially if you are doing this yourself.

The hindquarters provide the best quality roasts and steaks, and I hate to waste such fine, solid meat on grinding or jerky. Of course, this is a personal opinion, and if you and your family like jerky and ground meat best, prepare your meat the way you will eat it.

To remove the meat from the bones in the hindquarter, cut to the bone from the inside of the leg and peel the meat off and around the bone. The sirloin is located along the top and front of the hindquarter. Remove it by peeling off the entire muscle group while cutting lightly away at the connective tissue between the muscle groups. The sirloin contains two muscle groups: the top sirloin (the larger of the two) and the petite sirloin. These can be kept together for sirloin roasts or separated for steaks. Sirloin roasts can also be cut into fillets or steaks, depending on your preference.

The round muscle groups make up the bulk of the hind-quarters. The round is broken up into three muscle groups: the top round (medium in size), the bottom round (the largest), and the eye of the round (almost round in shape). These cuts make the finest roasts on wild game as well as fine steaks. Though the roasts can be cut into either fillets or steaks, fillets are the preferred form.

The remaining cut on the rear quarter is the shank, or the lower portion of the leg. The shank makes poor quality steaks but can be made into a roast. It also makes great ground meat because it contains a lot of flavor. You'll find the shank has a lot of connective tissue. It is fruitless to try to remove this tissue, which is why I recommend grinding it or keeping it for a slow-cooked roast. Any meat left on the hindquarter I cut up to bottle or fillet it into jerky slices. Remember the look of the steaks and roasts so that you can label them when you're wrapping and packaging them.

The back straps and the tenderloins are the easiest to cut up, which is why I do them last. They can be cut across the grain into steaks or left in large portions as a filleted roast. You can cut your loin steaks as thick as you would like; I recommend two to three inches thick. The tenderloin is the signature cut on any animal and should be your finest cuts. Make sure that you cut so the grain is straight. The tenderloins make a very fine fillet roast.

How do I package my game meat?

After you are through cutting up your game, it is time to package it—the most important step in the process to ensure your meat lasts in the freezer. Freezer burn is a real threat and ruins more game meat than anything else. Freezer burn happens when the temperature of the freezer fluctuates, which always happens, and the outside layers of the meat thaw out and then refreeze. This process causes moisture from that portion of the meat to be drawn out, forming ice and leaving the meat dry. The moisture drawn out of the meat continues to thaw and freeze, tainting the flavor as it does. When you open a thawed piece of freezer-burned meat, you will immediately be met with an unpleasant smell. Most meat at this point will be thrown to the dogs.

This is why I cut most of my meat into roasts. Roasts have less air space surrounding them, allowing less moisture to be drawn out from the meat. If the meat does freezer burn, it is easier to recover. Simply cut off the bad part of the meat and cook the rest.

In the earlier part of the last century, an intact mammoth was found under the ice of the Arctic. Science at the time was not as advanced as it is now, so the carcass was not immediately seized upon by people studying the Ice Age. Instead, a lot of the meat was cut out and sold in restaurants in New York City. Reports claimed the meat tasted excellent, despite being literally thousands of years old.

This illustrates the principle that when meat is protected from air it will not freezer burn. Steaks freezer burn so easily because it is impossible to remove all the air from between the steaks if they are packaged together. Once a steak is freezer burned, you have to cut away most of it to have edible meat left. When I thaw out my roasts, I cut them into steaks or whatever I want. I have eaten game packaged this way that was three years old, and it tasted great.

To package your meat, begin by wrapping the meat in plastic and removing the air. A vacuum sealer is the best method to use; most sealers remove 99 percent of the air. Vacuum sealers cost between fifty and one hundred dollars, but they are well worth the money for the difference they make in the quality of your meat.

If you don't have a vacuum sealer, plastic wrap works fine. The wrap should be the variety that clings to itself, such as Saran Wrap. Lay a sheet of plastic wrap on a flat surface, then lay the chunk of meat at the top of the sheet and roll it, folding over the sides until it is completely covered. If any meat is uncovered, wrap the cut again until it is completely covered.

Plastic wrap works well because you can eliminate most of the air if you wrap the piece tightly. I have yet to find a plastic bag that wards off freezer burn; I've never been able to remove all the air when packaging meat in plastic bags.

After the meat has been vacuum packed or plastic wrapped, wrap it in butcher paper. You can find this paper almost anywhere, and I consider it a must in preserving my meat. Cut off a square section of the butcher paper and place your meat on the corner of the sheet. Then roll it towards the opposite corner. When you have wrapped it three-quarters of the way, tuck in the paper on the sides and finish rolling to the end. Seal up the roll with a strip of masking tape.

Mark the date and cut of meat on the outside of the package with a black permanent marker so you can easily identify pieces when you need them. I haven't always marked my meat, and more than once I've thawed out a package of dog scraps when I was anticipating steaks!

Also, when it comes time to cook your meat, thaw it out on its own if at all possible. Your meat will have a much better taste. The microwave seems to transfer some of the freezer flavor into the meat itself, causing the flavor to be off a little. Plan ahead the night before or at least the morning before you plan to cook the meat and pull it out of the freezer. Place it in the fridge to thaw. You will be much more satisfied with the results.

How do I bottle my meat?

To bottle meat, make sure all the pieces are similar in size and shape. You can find mason jars at most grocery stores, discount stores, or stores devoted to food preservation. Fill jars to the top with the meat; it will shrink 25–35 percent when bottled. You don't need to add any spices, although I like to include a teaspoon of salt and a dash of onion powder.

Once the meat is packed into the bottle, place the lid on top and secure the twist ring in place. Seal the lids by placing the bottles in a large pressure cooker, then cook. Process an hour for pint size bottles; quart bottles take an hour and a half. If there is any doubt about the time needed, refer to the guidelines that come with your pressure cooker. Pressure cookers are fairly expensive, but if you plan to bottle much meat, they will be a worthwhile investment. You can often find pressure cookers at yard sales or second-hand stores at quite a discount. I'm always on the lookout for them and have found them for as little as thirty dollars.

Once meat is bottled, it lasts for years as long as the seal isn't broken. Many people who are short on freezer space choose to bottle meat. Bottled meat is very tender and works wonderfully in sandwiches, stews, and other similar dishes.

When I was growing up, my best friend and I went on a horse-back adventure through the mountains of central Utah almost every Saturday. We always packed a bottle of elk meat and home-made cookies for lunch. We dug up wild onions to supplement our feast and ate the meat straight out of the bottle. It saddens me to see that bottled meat is becoming a thing of the past. For generations, it was the only way to effectively preserve meat. Try bottling meat once, and I promise you will do it again.

How do I grind my meat?

Of course, a meat grinder isn't an essential for this method, but if you have one, it's a breeze. Quality meat grinders cost between seventy-five and two hundred dollars, and, once again, if you plan on eating a lot of ground meat, the grinders are definitely worth every penny. Many people take meat to a butcher and have it ground up there. By the time you pay seventy-five cents a pound, you'll find it adds up fast. It doesn't take long to pay more for that than a grinder would have cost.

There's no real secret to grinding meat; you simply push it through the grinder. The biggest complaint people have with ground venison is the flavor. Meat shops often add beef suet to the meat when they grind it to help the meat stick together. The problem is that beef suet and the fats in venison do not mix well. Pork fat is a much better option because it blends well with the flavor of venison. Of course, you don't have to add anything. If you have problems with your ground venison sticking together for burger patties, add a little molasses to the meat before you cook it.

You'll find lots of ways to use your meat once it is ground. You can use it straight, make it into sausages, or fix up a ground-jerky product; you'll find several delicious recipes in the recipe section of this book. Whichever option you choose, package and freeze your ground meat immediately.

How do I make jerky?

Jerky comes in two types: slab jerky and ground, or pressed, jerky. The first step is deciding which type you want to make.

You'll find there's no secret to making great-tasting jerky—it's simply dried meat. For hundreds of years, jerky was the only way to preserve meat. Refrigerators were a miracle for the future, and even bottling meat was unheard of. Dried meat, however, could last for a long time without spoiling. Many people dried their meat with wood smoke to add flavor and to ward off bacteria.

The Native Americans of the plains made stockpiles of buffalo jerky to last them through the harsh winters when it was hard to hunt and meat was desperately needed for strength and warmth. They often boiled the jerky in a soup to stretch the valuable meat even further. Today, jerky is more a treat than anything else. When I make jerky in my house, we are lucky if it lasts through the month.

As I said before, there is no right or wrong way to make jerky. You can make jerky with nothing on it at all or add lots of spices. If you spice jerky, you can opt for marinade or a rub.

To make slab jerky, cut strips with the grain an eighth of an inch thick. You can make this process easier by using a meat cutter. Set the cutter thickness, and cut the meat lengthwise. You can also build a jerky block by nailing two strips of wood to the sides of a chunk of 2x4 wood. The strips of wood should be an eighth of an inch above the 2x4. Set the meat on the block of wood, and run a sharp knife across the wood to slice off the jerky. Most often, I cut my jerky strips directly off the carcass as I butcher my deer.

Start your marinade with a base; soy sauce and Worcestershire sauce are the two most common bases because of their flavor and availability. Beer and sodas make fine bases as well, as does Italian Dressing. Once you've selected a base, add spices. Taste your marinade as you go; your jerky will taste like your marinade, only slightly more subtle.

I love to use the marinades by McCormick's Seasonings. You can find them almost anywhere, and they are very affordable, often costing less than a dollar.

Once your marinade is complete, add your meat and let it soak for several days in the refrigerator. Stir it often until the color of the marinade soaks through the meat. When the meat has been properly marinated, dry it by air, a food drier, a smoker, or even an oven set at a low temperature. Check your meat often while it is drying. If it overdries, the jerky will taste burnt. Jerky is done when the outside is glossy in color and the meat is still somewhat pliable, not crispy.

Either vacuum pack jerky or place it in a plastic bag. Then freeze it until you want to use it. Freezing isn't necessary, but it does preserve the flavor and make the jerky last longer.

If you are using a rub, start with a sugar cure base. Very affordable, sugar cure is available in most grocery stores in the baking goods aisle and helps preserve your meat. To make your rub, blend any spices you want into the sugar cure. Be creative and have fun creating your own recipes. As the name implies, a rub is massaged into the meat. After you have rubbed it in, dry the meat as you would marinated jerky.

Ground jerky eliminates the prep work of cutting the jerky, and it also utilizes ground meat that you might otherwise not use. Follow the same basic steps as slab jerky to make ground jerky. When you marinade the ground meat, use a lot less marinade than you would with slab meat. Soak the meat until the marinade is absorbed. When the marinade is absorbed, use a jerky-making gun to squirt the meat onto racks for drying. You can also place the marinated meat into a plastic bag and cut one corner, then squeeze the meat out as you would frosting.

When making ground jerky, you must use a food drier or smoker. The meat will go bad if you try to air dry it and it will simply cook like a burger in the oven.

When you make jerky, do not put all your eggs in one basket. Have fun and experiment until you find the type you like best. Once you find the type you like, play with the flavor. Venison jerky is a healthy snack and very inexpensive. When you are camping or hunting, jerky provides an excellent source of nutrition and tastes better than energy bars. Jerky contains the fats and proteins you need for a constant supply of energy.

Cooling the meat during warm-weather hunts can be a challenge. Photo courtesy of Randy Judd

Ten Secrets to Cooking Venison

When I was growing up, we depended on the venison we harvested as our main meat source. The venison I ate growing up tasted great and always gave me energy. The meat was rich in flavor and very moist, far superior to any beef I have ever had.

On the other hand, some of the worst-tasting meat I ever ate was venison served at friends' homes. This meat was dry and tough with an overwhelming liver-like flavor. I understood quickly why so many people turned up their nose at venison.

Some people don't care what happens to an animal after harvesting it. Some meat cutters tell stories of waking up and having deer or elk left on their porches, either at work or at home! This practice is both irresponsible and despicable. To waste such fine meat is terrible thing to do. Why kill the animal in the first place?

Cooking venison and other wild game is an art form that has been all but lost with modern-day developments. We don't prepare meals as we used to. Our food trends have moved from the homemade to the already prepared, and what cooking we actually do often depends heavily on recipes. This is where a lot of the art is lost. Traditional cooking methods were often a matter of tasting and experimenting, rather than following specific recipes.

Learning to cook venison on your own can be challenging. However, I've learned many things through the years as I've worked to perfect the art of cooking venison. My dad prepared great-tasting venison, but he stuck to a simple approach: fried in a skillet with onions, salt, and pepper. This is a great way to cook venison, but I felt compelled to learn more. Some of my experiments tasted terrible, but others weren't so bad. I had a lot of venison to practice with, and I had the determination to do so. Interestingly enough, the worst recipes I found were in cookbooks. The meat often tasted stale and turned out dry. I wondered why. I followed the recipes exactly. Even the recipes I found in wild-game cookbooks tasted terrible.

Eventually, I learned that cooking venison is a process. Directions exist as general guidelines, but I learned to experiment and play with recipes, applying the wisdom I had gained through my own experience. Some of the best instruction I received was from my next-door neighbor. I spent many evenings with this older gentleman, watching old John Wayne movies, sharpening knives, and learning to cook venison. He never used a recipe, which intrigued me, but his meals were always exquisite. He possessed the secrets that I wanted so badly: the secrets to cooking venison.

For the past fifteen years I have experimented and learned from what he and my dad taught me, and I feel that I've also discovered the secrets to cooking great-tasting venison. I have learned how and why cooking venison is different from cooking other meats, and I'm eager to share these tips with you. If you follow these instructions carefully, you'll find that the recipes I've provided are wonderful guidelines, but you'll be creating dishes of your own every time you cook.

How do I learn to cook venison?

A key to cooking great venison is understanding what venison is. Sounds simple, but so many people don't take the time to make the distinction. The reason many of my early experiments failed is that the recipes I was following were written for cooking domestic meat. Domestic meat and venison differ greatly from each other, and you can't cook them the same way and enjoy the same results. Wild game and domestic meat have a number of significant differences in their composition.

The number one way these two types of meat differ is in the muscle type. This does not refer to the color of the meat. Chicken and pork are often called white meat, and beef and venison are often called red meat. Here I refer to the type of muscle itself. Domestic meat is made up mostly of white muscle tissue; wild game is made up of mainly red muscle tissue.

Of course, all animals have both types of muscle tissue. When you have a turkey for Thanksgiving dinner, the red and white muscle tissue difference is very noticeable. The leg meat, often called dark meat, is composed of red muscle tissue, and the breast meat, often called white meat, is composed of white muscle tissue. Most people like one better than the other. Dark meat tends to be more flavorful and moist than white meat.

Both genetics and activity play a role in determining what type of muscle tissue an animal has. A wild turkey doesn't look the same as a domestic turkey. The domestic turkey has been bred specifically to have a large plump breast, as this is the most desired meat. Most domestic turkeys can only fly a short distance, if at all. On the other hand, a wild turkey has a longer, leaner breast that is darker in color and richer in flavor. The wild turkey flies reasonably well and is composed mainly of red muscle tissue.

We can also see an example of this in humans. On a football team, linemen boast bulky, heavy muscles capable of a great amount of energy released in short bursts, all indicative of white muscle tissue. Receivers, on the other hand, have built long, lean muscles capable of extended running and speed—features of red muscle tissue.

Red muscle tissue is built when muscles are used for speed and endurance. Animals such as deer and elk are composed of up to 90 percent red muscle tissue. These animals are built to run fast for long periods of time to elude their predators. Their very nature gives them the genetic coding to create red muscle tissue. Red muscle tissue is not capable of releasing extreme amounts of energy in one large burst; rather, these muscles release controlled amounts of energy for long periods. Red muscle fibers are long and lean in shape with highly concentrated amounts of proteins. Fats in red muscle contain small amounts of mainly monounsaturated fats, which are both healthy and essential for your body.

White muscle tissue occurs when muscles are used for short, massive bursts of energy. Mountain lions are prime examples of animals composed of mainly white muscle tissue. These animals are capable of amazing bursts of energy; they can leap thirty feet in a single jump. However, they cannot run for long distances as a deer can.

Most of our domestic meat animals are composed of white muscle tissue because white muscle tissue is heavier and bulkier than red muscle tissue. Because meat is sold by weight, this means the meat producer makes a larger profit on white-muscle animals.

This wasn't always the case. The Texas Longhorns that are such an icon of the American West were composed chiefly of red muscle tissue. A market-ready Longhorn steer was half the weight of a present-day beef steer. However, with the advent of feedlots and rail yards, beef producers started breeding for a heavier, shorter beef animal.

White muscle fibers are short and thick in diameter. A white muscle fiber has less protein strands attached than a red muscle fiber does. They also contain a large amount of saturated fats, which are difficult for your body to digest and can cause lasting health problems including obesity and heart attacks.

These differences are important to learn and note. This is why using recipes and methods of cooking from a standard cookbook will not work when cooking wild game. The different muscle types react differently when you cook them. Many people get frustrated when they cook wild game because the meat doesn't turn out as good as the domestic meat they cook. Just keep in mind that you wouldn't cook salmon the same way you'd cook pork, so why would you cook venison the same way you'd cook beef?

Fat is what gives any meat its flavor. Without fat, meat is quite bland. This is why you don't see round steaks on the dinner menu at a fancy steak house. Round steak is extremely low in fat and therefore low in flavor. On the other hand, a New York or rib eye steak contains a high amount of fat and is very flavorful.

Do you know why everything tastes like chicken? Chicken

breast meat has almost no fat of any kind, so chicken breast meat itself is extremely bland. Because they have almost no flavor of their own, chicken breasts taste like whatever you season them with. A lot of people who don't like meat will eat chicken, claiming that it doesn't taste like meat. Interestingly enough, these same people won't eat chicken legs, because chicken legs contain fat—and flavor!

When you cook meat high in saturated fats, the heat from the cooking transforms these fats from a solid to a liquid. The liquid fat then flavors and moistens the meat. This process is similar to putting Crisco in a pan then heating it up on the stove. As the pan heats up, the Crisco begins to melt into a liquid.

The problem with saturated fats is that your body needs to break them down before it can use them. When they arrive in the body in this state, the body simply transfers these fats directly to storage, where they will stay unless the body needs to break them down for energy. When you eat a high amount of saturated fats, you feel sluggish and worn out because your body is working so hard to break these fats down for use. Eating saturated fats produces high levels of LDL cholesterol.

The unsaturated fats in wild game are already broken down and ready for immediate use. After you eat unsaturated fats, you have instant energy that will sustain you for some time. The trick to cooking wild game is preserving these fats. If you can learn to keep these fats in the meat, you will have great-tasting venison.

SECRET #1—Preserve the fats in the meat

So how do you do this? Venison and all wild game have to be cooked in one of two ways: Slow and low (cooked slow at a low temperature) or hot and fast (cooked fast at a high temperature). Either of these two methods will keep as much of the fat as possible in the meat.

When you cook meat hot and fast, you sear the ends of the meat and allow the inside of the meat to cook to a proper temperature without losing the fats and moisture. When you cook a steak in a pan that is not hot enough, the fats and moisture in the meat will be lost. As the pan heats up, the heat transfers into the meat, and the moisture is extracted out to regulate this heat exchange. If the pan is at a high enough temperature, the meat seals itself immediately upon touching the hot surface.

When you are hot cooking venison, your cooking temperature should be between five hundred and eight hundred degrees. You don't need a thermometer to check for this temperature. Hold your hand a few inches above the heat source. If you cannot hold your hand for three seconds, it is hot enough to sear the meat. These temperatures are easily reached on a grill or in a skillet on your stove.

This is critical to cooking good venison; I believe that it is one of the main mistakes people make. Too often venison turns out dry and tough, but it doesn't need to be, and this is the step that makes the difference. Once the meat is sealed, you can cook it as long as you like until it is done according to your desires.

When you slow cook venison, you should cook it at a temperature between one hundred and sixty-five and two hundred degrees for an extended period of time. This is hot enough to kill off all the bacteria but cool enough that the moisture will not boil off because it is below boiling temperature.

The seasonings that you use on your meat are not nearly as important as this process for achieving good results. Preserving these fats is the number one thing you can do to enjoy great-tasting venison.

The fats in venison all have a different flavor, depending on the particular area where the animal was taken. However, although there are differences, you'll also find a lot of similarities in the meat. I would compare it to flavor of a Pacific king salmon compared to that of an Atlantic salmon. They both taste like salmon, but they offer slight differences in taste as well.

Much of the difference can be attributed to differences in diet, or what the animals eat. The fats that affect the taste the most are the saturated fats, and these flavors are not always pleasing; for many palates they are a little strong sometimes. Trim off any visible fat before cooking the meat to reduce these strong flavors.

SECRET #2—Use a small amount of oil in your pan

This is absolutely essential when you are cooking venison in a skillet. If you do not use oil, you will be left with dry meat every time. When you cook beef or pork in a skillet, the saturated fats render down and provide the buffer, or the medium, to allow the heat to transfer from the pan to the meat. Oil is not necessary because the amount of saturated fat in the meat makes up for this need.

However, wild game in general, and venison in particular, has so little fat that it is necessary to provide a buffer to allow the heat transfer. If you don't do this, the moisture and the fats will be extracted from the meat and cause the meat to be bland and dry. To make matters worse, these fats burn easily and cause a bad flavor, often referred to as a gamey flavor, to penetrate the meat. You do not need to use very much oil, just enough to cover the bottom of the pan.

If you are cooking on a grill, oil is unnecessary.

Generally speaking, when we cook roasts we use a Crock-Pot, Dutch oven, or baking dish, and we often add a sauce. In these instances, the sauce acts as a medium for transferring the heat, so oil is unnecessary. If you try to cook a roast without a sauce, you will be left with dry meat. This doesn't mean that you need a lot of liquid; you certainly don't want to boil your meat. You only need enough liquid or oil to allow the transfer of heat.

I have also had a lot of people ask about using rotisseries for cooking venison roasts. Most of them who have tried rotisseries ended up with very dry meat. Generally speaking, the majority of rotisseries on the market do not generate enough heat to seal the meat properly. This problem can be fixed simply by searing the meat in a hot pan on all sides before putting it on the rotisserie. Also, wrapping the meat in bacon beforehand keeps it moist as well. If meat is sealed before being placed on the rotisserie, rotisseries do a fine job of cooking meat. If you have a commercial rotisserie that reaches five hundred degrees, this temperature should be sufficient. Cook the meat at full heat for ten to fifteen minutes, then turn the temperature down and finish cooking the meat to your satisfaction.

SECRET #3—Learn to cut the meat correctly

This doesn't sound like a big deal, but it makes a huge difference in how meat cooks. Unlike beef, with venison it does not matter where the cut of meat comes from nearly as much as how the meat is cut.

Cuts of beef differ by the amount of fat. Beef rounds have very little fat and, therefore, are tough and bland. Rib cuts, on the other hand, are full of fat and are tender and moist. Venison contains very little saturated fat, so most of the meat cooks the same regardless of where it is cut off the animal. This is a different way of thinking for people who are used to dealing with beef.

So, if cut matters, what kind of cut do you want? If the steak is cut with the grain straight up and down, the meat cooks a lot better than if it is cut on an angle. This is because of a process called capillary action. Muscle fibers are tubular in shape and are made up of protein strands bound together by fine "hairs." The inside of the muscle fibers are full of water and fats.

When the heat enters the meat, it fills and transfers through the tube-like fibers from the source on up. The shorter the distance the heat has to travel through the fiber, the quicker the meat will cook, and the least amount of fat will be lost. Also the straight-cut muscle fibers can be broken apart much easier on a vertical bite or cut.

In other words, the straighter the cut, the more tender the meat. If you are cutting the meat yourself this is something that you always need to watch for. One thing that bothers me is people complaining about the job that meat cutters do. People tell me all the time that meat they received back from the meat cutter was not theirs, or else it was bad when they got it back. I know a lot of meat cutters, and I have to say that 99 percent of the time it is the field care, not the cutter, that made a difference in the meat. Most meat cutters are extremely professional and will cut your meat with your best interest in mind. Keep in mind that, if you do not receive the exact same amount of meat that you brought in, most meat cutters carve off and dispose of meat that is bloodshot, bruised, or otherwise tainted.

If you are cooking meat as a roast, the cut is not nearly as important as with steaks. Roasts generally take longer to cook than steaks, and after they are done, they will be cut up into individual-sized pieces. Stew meat is one of the worst fresh cuts you can have with venison, and I don't ever recommend it. The pieces are so small that when you cook stew meat, all the fats and moisture extract themselves from the meat before it has a chance to seal. The only way to have tender stew meat from a fresh cut is to cook it slowly for a long time, which ruins the integrity of the venison flavor and is not recommended. As far as cuts of meat to use in stews or soups, bottled meat is far better than any other cut of meat. If you insist on using a fresh cut of meat, I'd suggest slow cooking a roast in your stew, and cutting it up right before the stew is ready to be served.

What if you want to stir fry your venison or try venison fajitas? Try cooking the meat first as a steak, separate from the other ingredients, then cut it into strips and add it to the other ingredients. This provides you tender meat while still retaining the integrity of the flavor of your meat.

Truly elegant dishes are not the typical cowboy dish where everything is thrown in together and it all tastes the same. Elegant dishes are tasty offerings where individual ingredients retain their flavors while blending together in beautiful harmony as you eat them. If you keep that in mind as you cook your venison dishes, you will be surprised how well they will taste.

SECRET #4—Learn how long to cook the meat

Overcooked venison turns more people away from venison than almost anything. My guess is that, among those who over-cook venison, half of the chefs simply don't recognize when the meat is done, while the other half are afraid of getting sick from wild game so they want to make sure it is well cooked. It amazes me that many people will eat a bloody, rare beef steak but won't touch venison unless it's burned.

In fact, wild meat is much cleaner and healthier to eat. Wild animals eat clean food, live in clean air, and have room to run as they wish. A deer or elk harvested on the mountain contains no artificial growth hormones or dyes in the meat. To say it simply: venison is a clean, healthy meat source.

Those who cook venison too long out of ignorance simply haven't learned how to cook it properly. First, you don't use the same indicators that you would use when cooking beef. Venison is made up of red muscle tissue, which is darker in color than white muscle tissue. If you were to set a beef steak and an elk steak side-by-side, the elk steak would be several shades darker. A beef steak is cooked medium according to the color indicators, which means that the internal temperature of the meat has reached 163 degrees for longer than one minute. Well-done venison steak resembles a medium-rare beef steak because it starts out so much darker. Most people do not know this and ignorantly overcook their venison.

When meat is overcooked, proteins that make up the muscle fibers coagulate and bind together, resulting in meat that is tough and dry. This happens regardless of the type of meat you are cook-ing. In addition, people often cut into the meat to check the color for doneness. This is a mistake. Even with a small cut, essential fats and juices that were sealed into the meat when you seared it seep out. Once the meat has cooled off a little, you can make a small cut in the meat and no moisture will be lost.

So how do you know when meat is done? A simple process called sweating the meat. After the meat has been seared, cook it until a layer of moisture, or what I call sweat, forms on the top of the steak. When the sweat appears, that means the heat has penetrated fully and pushed some of the juices out of the meat. When the meat sweats, it's time to turn it over.

When the meat has sweated two times, the meat is cooked to the rare stage. Pull it off the grill or stove at this point if you like medium-rare steak. Sweating the meat three times will leave the meat at medium rare. Pull it off at this point if you like a medium steak. Sweating the meat four times means the meat is well done. You should never cook venison beyond this point, so take it off the grill or stove.

All wild game has a residual heat factor that you need to consider. This means that even after you take the meat off the grill it will continue to cook for a few minutes. If you cook your wild meat beyond four sweats, the residual heat factor means the proteins will continue to coagulate and the meat will become tough.

Personally, I rarely cook my meat more than two sweats, and I always end up with tender, flavorful meat. You'll be amazed at how well this process works. In fact, once you become familiar with the sweat method, you won't ever need to cut into meat again to see what it looks like.

Now, it's important to have your meat the same relative thickness. If one end of your steak is thin and the other is thick, the sweating method isn't nearly as effective. In fact, regardless of which method you use, you're likely to end up with some overcooked and some undercooked meat.

SECRET #5—Learn when to season the meat

Seasoning your meat is a critical, often overlooked, step to cooking meat. Many people spice their meat before placing it on the grill. If you want moist, juicy meat, try a different approach.

Seasonings block the path of heat when you seal and sear your meat, so wait to add seasonings until the meat has been seared. Once your meat has been seared on one side, turn it over and add your seasonings. You can add additional seasonings when you turn your meat over a second time. Your meat will have just as much flavor as meat that is flavored from the very beginning—and your meat will be effectively sealed and seared, so it will be moist and flavorful.

Also, the sweating process described earlier works to bind the seasonings to the meat. This is a secret of cooking meat known by chefs worldwide that is not generally known among the public, although I'm not certain why. It's a simple concept, and it makes sense.

The only exception to this is when you use a marinade. I don't recommend a marinade for a small cut of venison, such as a steak. When you marinade a beef steak, the juices from the marinade break down the saturated fats, and the juices and fats bind together.

When the meat is cooked and the fats begin to render and flavor the meat, the marinade also releases its flavor into the meat. Because venison has so few saturated fats, the marinade actually breaks down and extracts the unsaturated fats from the meat, meaning that you lose the natural flavor of the meat, and the meat ends up being quite dry.

If you are cooking a large roast, you can use a marinade to replace some of the fats on the outside layer because the inside layers of meat will keep the fats intact. However, every time I have tried marinating a venison steak I am left with dry, bland meat.

Learning what types of seasonings to use on different types of venison can be valuable. Salt is the number one seasoning used but, in my book, using salt is a cop-out. Besides being all too ordinary, high levels of salt are not good for you. As you try different seasoning combinations and less salt, you'll be amazed at the results. Your meat tastes better and will be healthier for you.

Learning to season meat is not something that you will perfect overnight. I've taken years to experiment and learn what seasonings taste best with various types of venison. For example, I use a sweeter, milder seasoning for antelope to complement this sweet and mild meat. On the other hand, for an oak-filled whitetail I would opt for a bold, slightly acidic seasoning, such as Italian dressing, to complement the relatively bold taste of acorns.

You'll find plenty of recipes that go well with just about every type of venison. Experiment with different ideas and come up with favorite recipes of your own. I hope I've offered you basic guidelines and you can discover your own tricks. That is half of the fun of cooking wild game.

SECRET #6—Let the meat thaw on its own

I know this sounds insignificant, but it is not. Microwave ovens may be one of the best inventions of the past century, but they are horrible for wild game. The microwave cooks by sending high-frequency radio waves through the object being heated. When the waves go through the object, friction heats up the object from the inside. These waves alter fats in meat and bind proteins, causing the meat to be tough. This rule applies to all meat, both domestic and wild. However, it is especially harmful to the unsaturated fats in the wild game.

The other disadvantage is the frozen moisture on the outside of the meat. This moisture will be saturated with any outside influence from your freezer. Just like ice cubes left in a freezer for a while, this frozen layer will take on a freezer taste. When you thaw out meat naturally, this moisture drains off without affecting the meat. When you microwave the meat, the moisture is pushed into the meat, giving it that older, freezer taste.

Plan your meals so you have time to set meat in the fridge the night before so it can thaw out naturally. This single step goes far in ensuring that your meat is moist and flavorful.

SECRET #7—Use cast iron cookware

In recent years, Dutch oven cooking has become a popular pastime, especially in the West. Just saying the words "Dutch oven" can start plenty of mouths salivating.

What makes Dutch oven cooking so good? It is the cast iron

cookware. In fact, cast iron cookware provides plenty of qualities that make it ideal for cooking both in the home and outdoors. The number one reason cast iron pots are ideal for cooking venison is that they are the only cookware able to withstand the extreme temperatures used for cooking wild meat.

Venison steaks should be cooked at five hundred to eight hundred degrees, a level of temperature that most pots cannot withstand. When Teflon pans get too hot, the Teflon flakes off, leaving little black specks in your meat. Light stainless steel and aluminum pans warp when they get too hot. Cast iron withstands the high temperatures and also eliminates hot spots when the pan has been seasoned properly.

Seasoning a cast iron pan is not difficult. After you buy a new pan, wash it well with soap and water; I even let it sit in water overnight. You can also burn out a new pan in a fire to get rid of the packing grease. Once you've cleaned the pan, season it by heating it up in an oven or on the fire. Then work oil into the pan several times while it is hot.

The pan begins to really take the seasoning after you cook with it the first time. The more you cook with your cast iron pan, the better seasoned it becomes. You'll find there's no substitute for a well-seasoned cast iron pan. I love to use my cast iron cookware on campouts. I use a Camp Chef 30,000 BTU burner that will heat up my pans to 500 to 800 degrees in just a matter of seconds. No other type of pan is able to withstand that quick heat exchange.

Most people have a cast iron skillet and don't like to use it because it's too heavy and everything sticks to it. The weight will always be an issue, but that is part of what makes the skillet so good. The weight allows the pan to stay put while you cook and not warp at high temperatures. But the sticking complaint is real; everything *does* stick to a cast iron pan that hasn't been seasoned. Cast iron is an alloy, made of 95 percent iron, 2 percent silicon, and 1 percent manganese. It has a pebbly surface because it is cast in a sand mold.

Remember in my earlier discussion how I mentioned that

heat transfer occurs better when there is an oil to buffer the heat transfer? The season in the cast iron works as that critical buffer. The heat transfer with the oil buffer will be even across the pan so you don't have hot spots.

Many old cast iron pans don't work very well because they have been washed with dish soap. Dish soap is the absolute worst thing for a cast iron pan. Dish soap breaks down and binds to oils so they can be removed from the pan. With a cast iron pan, this is exactly what you don't want happening! Without these oils, the pans have hot spots, and the thirsty, clay-filled pores of the pan try to absorb oil from the meat, which usually causes the meat to stick.

The best way is to clean out your pan is to rinse it with water while it is still hot. Most everything should rinse right out. If there are some stubborn spots, scour them out with a scrub brush or a scouring pad. When the pan is rinsed out, wipe it out with a paper towel, and you are done. You can also wipe it out with a little oil, which helps season in pan. Don't worry about whether or not the pan is clean. The oil layer, or season, of the pan prevents anything from saturating into the pan itself.

A Dutch oven seals in all of the juices and moisture with its thick, heavy lid. Also, thanks to the lid, Dutch ovens can cook things for a long time on relatively low heat. Meats slow cooked in a Dutch oven are almost always flavorful and moist. You can find a number of interesting and informative books on Dutch oven cooking.

Whether or not you become serious about Dutch oven cooking or simply do it on occasion, you'll find it to be a fun hobby. Whether you use a Dutch oven or just a cast iron skillet, once you learn to use cast iron pans, you will become convinced of their effectiveness.

SECRET #8—Use vinegar

I always keep an inexpensive bottle of white vinegar around my kitchen; it's an extremely versatile item to have on hand. If I pull out some meat from the freezer and there's a small amount of freezer burn on the steak, a quick dip in vinegar kills the bad taste. I learned this tidbit from my next-door neighbor in Levan, Utah. Any time meat had freezer burn, he poured a little vinegar on a plate and let the steak sit in it for a couple of minutes. I rely on this trick, and it works wonders to freshen up meat that has been in the freezer for a while.

Don't misunderstand me! I certainly don't want to imply that you should have your meat swimming in vinegar! The by-product of blood breaking down in your meat can be neutralized and counteracted by small amounts of vinegar, that's all.

You can even use vinegar if your meat doesn't have a fresh smell when you open the packages. That old-venison smell turns more people off of venison than almost anything else, yet the meat is still perfectly fine. A little vinegar or lemon juice brings back the taste wonderfully. Personally, I prefer white vinegar because it's mild flavor doesn't alter the flavor of the meat.

SECRET #9—Learn how to caramelize the meat

To caramelize meat means to physically change the composition of starches into sugars. This does not deal directly to composition of the meat, since meat is not made of either of these substances. It is a term, however, used for sauces often used on meat, as well as the edges of your meat.

The caramelized portion of meat has a lot of flavor and is what makes a fine roast or glazed steak. I use caramelizing for many things; one of the most common things I caramelize is onions. Onions are the number one seasoning in the world for flavoring meat, and most people agree that they taste better caramelized than raw. An added bonus is that onions are one of the healthiest vegetables you can eat; they're full of vitamins, minerals, and antioxidants.

Many people hate onions because they've only tried them raw. Raw onions are extremely potent and can be hard for the body to digest. Once an onion has been caramelized, the starches turn into sugars, and the whole onion takes on a new, sweet flavor. I rely on caramelized onions a lot in my recipes because of the sweetness that I can only get from a fine onion.

Caramelizing does not occur only with onions; you can also caramelize sauces for glazes and roasts. When you are cooking a roast, if you keep the liquid level too high, the meat will not caramelize but will become boiled meat, which always comes up short on flavor and texture. Whether you use a Crock-Pot, a Dutch oven, or a roasting pan, watch that your liquid never reaches more than a third of the way up the roast, and be sure to turn the roast every half hour. This keeps the meat in good shape and produces that caramelized effect you are looking for in your meat.

You'll have to try this a few times to get caramelizing down to a science; there's a fine line between a well-caramelized roast and a burnt one. However, if you watch your meat properly and don't let it dry out, it will taste great every time.

You can also caramelize steaks. When I use this term with steaks, I mean that I want my spices to caramelize onto the outside of my meat for an intense, glazed flavor rather than burn into the steak. You can achieve the caramelized effect whenever you use recipes that use garlic, onions, or brown sugar; these glazes give your meat a unique flavor that will please even the pickiest eaters.

I also use a lot of wine sauces in caramelizing roasts and steaks. The trick here, however, is not to burn them by placing your meat in a hotter pan for a shorter amount of time. This isn't a trick you'll learn overnight, but it's well worth learning. Have fun and play with different ideas until you achieve the tastes you like.

Keep these few hints in mind:

- It is best to use a little sauce at a time to caramelize.

- Often times when I want to caramelize a steak, I will cook the steak fully then remove it from the pan. I then make a caramelized sauce in the pan and add the steak back in again to give it that extra touch; take care not to overcook the steak.

SECRET #10—Have fun!

The single most important thing you can do as you polish and refine this newfound hobby. Love what you are doing and love what you are eating!

I am not the world's greatest expert on venison or the world's greatest cook. I simply love to cook venison and have fun doing it. Try out the suggestions I have given you. Once you learn them, have fun cooking and try your own variations. I love hearing people say that what they've learned from me has changed their opinion of venison. I love to hear that people are cooking their meat and serving it to their families—and their families are loving it!

We live in a time when the majority of people have the ability to buy meat. We do not depend on game meat as our ancestors did. When we hunt game, what are we hunting it for? I hope it's not for the simple act of killing. Harvesting an animal and taking a life should never be about the kill.

To be able to hunt as our ancestors did and provide food for our families are some of the greatest thrills and most rewarding things you can do in your lifetime. I feel joy every time I serve game meat to my family, knowing that I harvested and provided that meat for them. Have fun with cooking your venison, and you will enjoy every minute of it.

Now that you know the secrets to cooking venison, try them out. I know you will be satisfied with the results. And once you have learned them, share them with your friends. These shouldn't be secrets! I want everyone to be aware of these tips on cooking venison so that more people can enjoy what I have been enjoying for years.

Bitten by the hunting bug, the author's wife, Katie, with her first deer, taken in central Utah.

COOKING VENISON STEAKS

I love sitting down to a great-tasting steak dinner—it's my favorite thing in the world to eat! And an elk steak would be my steak of choice. There's nothing quite like savoring a thick, rare steak that you harvested yourself. That is why I have decided to start out the recipe section with cooking steaks.

Cooking a venison steak is different than cooking a beef steak. To begin with, you should always cook a venison steak at least twice the temperature you cook a beef steak. You should also cook a venison steak twice as fast as you cook a beef steak—twice as hot, twice as fast! This is because of the different fat types you are trying to preserve, which I've mentioned in previous chapters.

Preparing venison properly is also critical to how it tastes.

Begin by thawing out the meat on its own; I've mentioned several times how important this is in cooking your meat. After the meat is thawed out, inspect it for any silver tissue, fat, or bruising. Remove these before you cook your meat; they will taint the flavor. Decide how you are going to cook your meat and prepare the ingredients so they are easily available. The meat cooks quickly, and you don't want it burning while you're fumbling around the spice cabinets looking for garlic.

Choose from the three viable ways to cook venison steaks: in a skillet, on a grill, or on the broiler. I personally prefer the skillet method because I like to make sauces to go along with my meat. In my recipes, I will refer back to the processes discussed in this chapter.

Cooking in a skillet

I prefer to cook venison in a cast iron skillet—no other pan does a finer job. Cast iron skillets have no hot spots and can withstand the high temperatures needed to cook a venison steak to perfection.

Heat up a little oil in the skillet; I prefer to use canola oil for health reasons and because it is more stable than other oils. Heat the oil to the point that it begins to smoke a little. When the oil smokes, the temperature will be about five hundred or six hundred degrees—ideal for cooking venison.

When the oil begins to smoke, place the steaks in the pan as quickly as possible. Cook the steaks for about two minutes, and turn them over. The cooked side should be browned. Don't leave the meat longer than two minutes because then the pan will cool down, and the other side of the meat won't sear properly.

After the meat has been turned, add your spices. Cook the meat on this side until a layer of sweat (juices) appears on the top of the steak; the spices should also be moist. Now turn the meat over and repeat the process. When the meat has sweated twice, once on each side, it is medium rare. If you sweat it three times, it is medium, and four times is well-done. Don't ever cook venison more than four sweats; that will leave the meat dry and bland.

Once you've removed the meat from the pan, let it sit for two to three minutes before serving it. The residual heat in the meat will finish cooking the meat to the desired affect. After I remove the meat, I like to add liquid to the pan and create sauces and glazes to pour over the meat; you will see this in a number of my recipes.

Cooking on the grill

During the warm summer months, cooking on the grill presents wonderful opportunities. Nothing beats hanging out around a barbecue grill with your family and friends!

Any outdoor grill works for cooking venison, as long as it is hot enough. Begin by preheating your grill or lighting your charcoals at least twenty minutes before you're ready to begin. This ensures that the grill is hot enough to properly cook the meat. You'll know the grill has reached adequate temperatures when you are unable to hold your hand directly above the rack for more than three seconds. Make sure your grill reaches this temperature before cooking.

As with the directions for cooking with a skillet, let the meat cook for two or three minutes, then turn it over and start adding spices. Let the meat sweat before you turn it back over. Follow the same directions provided in the skillet section above in determining how long to cook your meat. Keep in mind this one difference: a grill retains heat a lot better than a skillet, so meat cooks quicker on the grill. I have seen many people walk away from perfectly tender meat on a grill only to return a few minutes later to deer steaks that you could shingle a roof with.

Cooking with a broiler

This is my least preferred way to cook venison steaks, and I only mention it because of its popularity. To cook steaks on a broiler begin by preheating the broiler (with the broiler pan) for ten minutes to ensure the full temperature. Set the steaks on the broiler pan and broil for five minutes. Turn the steaks over and season them. Broil two more minutes for medium rare, three minutes for medium, and four minutes for done.

A broiler is less exact than either a grill or skillet, and meat can end up dry because it doesn't get sealed and seared correctly. However, with these disadvantages, the broiler is the best way to cooked bacon-wrapped venison.

A lot of my recipes have a distinct southwestern flare. This is not because I am limited in my ability to prepare other types of dishes, but because I feel that American cooking, as a whole, does not have any recognition in the culinary world. Southwestern-style cooking is the one type of American cooking unique to the culture from where it came. I like to create the type of dishes you would have been served in a saloon or a cantina in the late 1800s. These dishes vary greatly from the northern Rocky Mountain mining towns to the Mexican ports. Most of these recipes I created myself experimenting with different ideas. I must admit that, cooking the way I do, it's hard to produce an exact recipe. I cook as a process rather than in proportions. I have, however, tried my best to create recipes for you to use. I hope you will experiment with them, as I have, and have fun. As you do, you will learn the art of cooking.

I also stress using real butter instead of margarine in my recipes. This is because they react differently when they cook. Margarine is a hydrogenized oil, meaning it is an oil that has been altered somewhat to retain a solid form. When it is heated up, it simply becomes an oil again. Thus you are only adding oil to the meat and it will leave an "oily" texture. On the other hand, butter is made from milk fat. When it is heated, it makes a fine confluence between the spice and the meat without the oily effect.

Also, I mention garlic in my recipes. In all these recipes, minced garlic (store-bought or preminced) can be substituted for fresh garlic. The proportions are one teaspoon of minced garlic to one clove or fresh garlic.

MESQUITE VENISON STRIPS

This recipe is probably one of my all-time favorite venison recipes. It has a little spice to it but is not overwhelming. This meal is suited best as a Tex-Mex style dish served with beans, rice, and tortillas.

1 lb. venison steaks

4 cloves garlic sliced or 4 tsp. minced garlic

1 package mesquite marinade mix (dry)

¼ stick butter

¼ c. Worcestershire sauce

In a cast iron skillet, heat up a little oil until it begins to smoke. Cook steaks as described earlier in the chapter, adding garlic and dry marinade mix liberally to steaks after they have been turned over. When meat has sweated twice, remove from pan. Add butter and Worcestershire sauce to the hot skillet. Remove skillet from heat. Cut steak lengthwise into strips and add back to sauce. Stir well. Serve immediately.

Gunslinger Steaks

Most likely, hotels in the old West served up this tasty treat. Simple yet flavorful, this meat was traditionally served with fried potatoes and onions. Who am I to mess with tradition? I recommend the same.

1 lb. venison steaks

1 large onion (sweet is best)

1 c. chopped mushrooms (any type)

2 tsp. coarse ground black pepper

¼ c. beer

Salt to taste

This recipe was traditionally cooked in a cast iron skillet. Begin by slicing up the onion into rings or slivers. Set half aside to fry with potatoes. Fry steak in a skillet, adding onions and pepper after the first turn. After the last turn, add mushrooms, salt, and beer. Cook for 2 minutes and serve.

SILVER SALOON STEAKS

This recipe has a little bite! I imagine this dish being served south of the border in a silver-mining town. It goes equally well Tex-Mex style or fried potatoes.

1 lb. venison steaks

1 medium onion

2 cloves sliced garlic or 2 tsp. minced garlic

1 tsp. cumin

1 jalapeno pepper, sliced

1 red bell or Anaheim pepper, chopped

¼ stick butter

4 Tbsp. cider vinegar

Cook the steaks either in a skillet or on the grill, adding salt to taste after meat has been seared. In a skillet or a heavy saucepan, fry garlic, onions, and peppers in a little oil. Fry until jalapeno slices begin to brown. Add cumin, vinegar, and butter. When butter melts, remove from heat, add to steaks, and serve.

SOUTHWEST STEAKS

This simple recipe is made even easier by the marinade mix packets. Southwest steaks go perfectly with rice and a dark-green vegetable for a more sophisticated taste. It also goes well with Dutch-oven potatoes and corn for an outdoor flare.

1 lb. venison steaks

1 packet southwest marinade mix (dry)

1 tsp. liquid smoke per steak

Salt to taste

Cook steaks in a skillet, on the grill, or over a campfire, adding southwest marinade mix liberally after steaks have been seared. Let meat sweat three times. Remove from heat, add liquid smoke, and serve.

BAJA STRIPS

*This recipe definitely has a lot of attitude! I created this recipe think-
ing of a beach party on the Baja. I recommend serving it in tortillas
with beans, sour cream, and salsa.*

1 lb. venison steaks

2 fresh limes

¼ c. tequila, aged, not distilled

2 Roma tomatoes, chopped

¼ c. pineapple, crushed

Salt to taste

Cook these steaks on a grill, adding the tequila, 1 lime (squeezed),
and salt after the meat has been seared. Chop tomatoes and mix
with pineapple in a large serving bowl. When meat is done, cut
into strips and squeeze lime over them. Add meat to tomatoes
and pineapple and serve.

CHUCKWAGON STEAKS

This recipe works wonderfully for camping because you can make it so easily. It goes well with Dutch-oven potatoes or beans. I usually reserve this recipe for camp dinners, but it is great anytime you want an outdoor meal.

1 lb. venison steaks

1 lb. bacon

1 large onion

Salt to taste

Black pepper to taste

1 drop hot sauce per steak (I prefer Tapatio or Tabasco Chipotle smoked)

Cut onion in half and peel halves apart into individual layers. Place onion on the top of the meat, and wrap with a slice of bacon. Hold bacon and onion in place with a skewer or a toothpick. Cook meat on a grill. Add salt, pepper, and hot sauce to meat when seared. Serve immediately.

VENISON FAJITAS

This fajita recipe tastes delicious; I'm certain it will be one the best-tasting fajitas you've ever tried.

1 lb. venison steaks

1 large sweet onion

1 large red or orange bell pepper

1 tsp. cumin

2 large limes, fresh

1 fresh jalapeno, minced (substitute Anaheim pepper if your mouth is sensitive)

2 cloves garlic, minced

1 tsp. oregano

2 Roma tomatoes, chopped

¼ stick butter

¼ c. fresh cilantro, chopped

Cut bell pepper into strips about ¼-inch wide and 2 inches long, making sure to remove veins and seeds; set aside. Cut onion into slivers the same size as pepper strips. Set aside with peppers. In a separate bowl, mix tomatoes, jalapenos, garlic, cilantro, oregano, and cumin. Cook meat in a cast iron skillet. Add salt to taste after steak has been seared. When steak has sweated twice, remove from pan and set aside. Add butter to pan, and melt it. When butter is melted, add onions and peppers. Cook until they start to brown a little. When they have browned, add tomato mixture. Fry for a few minutes. While vegetables are frying, cut meat into strips lengthwise. When vegetables have cooked for 3 to 5 minutes, add meat strips back, and remove from heat. Squeeze limes onto fajita mixture. Let stand for a few minutes and serve in traditional fajita style in flour tortillas with sour cream.

The process I have described does a couple of things for you. First, the meat will be tender and retain its own flavor. Second, the vegetables will all be cooked to the extent that they need to be cooked. The onions and peppers need a little more time to caramelize while the tomatoes and cilantro are best simply warmed up.

VENISON FAJITAS (SIMPLE)

This recipe is great for good fajitas when you are in a hurry or don't feel like cooking a gourmet meal.

1 lb. venison steak

1 large red bell pepper

1 large onion

1 fajita seasoning mix

¼ cube butter

Cut onion and pepper into ¼-inch wide strips, taking care to remove the veins and seeds of pepper. Set aside. In a large skillet, fry steaks. Season meat liberally with the seasoning packet after meat has been seared, but save a little for the vegetables. When meat has sweated twice, remove from pan and set aside. In the same pan, melt butter and fry onion and pepper together until browned. Add the remainder of seasoning packet to mix. Cut steak into strips, and add to peppers and onions. Remove pan from heat and serve.

BEACH-GRILLED STEAKS

This recipe is an outside-party favorite! It should be cooked on a grill and served with melons, corn on the cob, and a salad of sorts. It has a light summer flavor that all can enjoy.

1 lb. venison steaks

4 cloves garlic, sliced

1 mango, peeled and sliced

1 c. pineapple, chopped

1 orange, peeled and chopped

1 fresh lime

1 fresh avocado, chopped

½ c. fresh cilantro, chopped

1 Roma tomato, chopped

1 large red onion

Salt to taste

Make salsa by chopping up mango, pineapple, orange, avocado, and tomato into bite-size chunks. Add to a mixing bowl. Add cilantro, and squeeze lime over salsa. Mix lightly and set aside. Cut onion into rings. Cut garlic into slices, and insert into meat by cutting a small slit in steak and inserting garlic slice. Cook steaks on a grill. Season with salt when meat has been seared. Set onion rings on steaks as they cook, letting heat from the grill caramelize them. Do not cook meat any more than three sweats. When meat is done, serve with onion and a scoop of fruit salsa over the top.

Red-Rock Strips

This is not a recipe for wimps! This recipe has a kick to it and tastes great as taco meat or with fried potatoes. Whichever way you choose to go, this is a great meal for a guy's night out.

1 lb. venison steaks

1 small onion

5 Tbsp. hot sauce

2 Tbsp. vinegar

2 Tbsp. Italian dressing

1 cube or tsp. chicken bouillon

2 Tbsp. honey

Cook the steak in a cast iron skillet. Add onions to steaks after turning the first time. When steaks have sweated twice, remove from the pan, and set aside. Leave onion in the pan and add hot sauce, vinegar, honey, dressing, and bouillon. Cook for 5 minutes. Cut steak into strips, and add to sauce. Remove from heat and let stand for 2 minutes before serving.

COUNTRY-FRIED STEAK

This is a favorite Southern recipe traditionally served with mashed potatoes, gravy, and corn. Make either a white (milk) gravy or brown gravy to go with it.

1 lb. venison steaks

2 eggs, whipped

1 c. bread crumbs

Salt and pepper to taste

4 Tbsp. brown sugar

¼ c. vinegar

Begin by whipping eggs to three times their original volume. Pour vinegar onto a plate and roll steaks in it. Mix bread crumbs, salt, and pepper together. After steaks have been rolled in vinegar, dip them in the eggs and roll them in the bread crumbs. Heat up a fair amount of oil in a large skillet. Cook steaks in skillet, turning them once when breading is golden brown. Serve with potatoes and gravy.

VENISON STROGANOFF

This is a traditional dish from Russia. This recipe is the scratch recipe made with steak strips. Stroganoff can be served with rice, potatoes, or egg noodles. It goes best with green vegetables such as beans or broccoli. Stroganoff is very versatile and easy to make. A simple stroganoff recipe is in the ground venison recipe section.

1 lb. venison steaks

1 medium onion

1 c. of mushrooms, whole or halved

4 cloves of garlic, minced

2 tsp. black pepper

6 c. whole milk

2 c. sour cream

1 tsp. rosemary

6 Tbsp. cornstarch

Slice the onion into slivers and carmelize it in a skillet with a little butter or oil until brown. Set onions in a large saucepan over medium heat, and add milk. When milk begins to lightly boil, add mushrooms, garlic, black pepper, and rosemary. Simmer for about 30 minutes. In a cast iron skillet, cook steaks with a little oil. Let sweat two times, adding salt and pepper to taste when meat has been seared. When meat is done, set aside. Turn sauce mixture up to high heat. Put cornstarch in a cup and add water until cornstarch is fluid. Add water-cornstarch mixture to sauce a little at a time until it is a thick soup-like consistency. Turn mixture down to low and stir in sour cream. Cut meat into bite-size chunks, and add to mixture. Remove stroganoff from heat and let stand 2 to 3 minutes. Serve over rice, potatoes, or egg noodles.

CREAMED VENISON TIPS

This recipe has French origins and is best served with rice. This dish is very elegant, and I enjoy serving it when company comes for dinner.

1 lb. venison steaks

½ c. brown mushrooms, chopped

½ lb. fresh medium shrimp, raw

2 cloves garlic

1 fresh lemon

1 lb. fresh asparagus

1 red bell pepper

½ stick butter

1 c. white wine

1 c. sour cream

Begin by cutting red bell pepper into ¼-inch strips 1 inch long, making sure to remove veins and seeds. Chop asparagus into two-inch pieces, removing any woody or white pieces from stalks. Peel and devein shrimp. Put shrimp, asparagus, and red peppers in a bowl. Start cooking steaks in a skillet. When meat has sweated twice, remove from heat and set aside. In a large saucepan, melt butter on high heat, and add shrimp, peppers, and asparagus. Cook until shrimp is all the same color (red). Add wine and garlic to the pan, and turn heat to medium. Start cutting steak into bite-size strips. Remove pan from heat, and stir in venison strips, sour cream, and squeeze juice from lemon into sauce. Let sauce stand for 2 or 3 minutes before serving.

COCA-COLA VENISON TIPS OVER RICE

I am not even sure where the idea for this recipe came from. I have been cooking this recipe for a few years, tweaking it until I felt I had it just right. One thing is for sure: it is a crowd favorite! As the title suggests, serve this over rice. I also like to serve it with green vegetables, such as fresh green beans with balsamic vinegar.

1 lb. venison steaks

1 can Coca-Cola

¼ c. Worcestershire sauce

3 Tbsp. vinegar

¼ c. mushrooms, chopped

1 tsp. basil

2 cubes beef bouillon

1 c. water

1 medium onion

3 cloves garlic, minced

3 Tbsp. liquid smoke

6 Tbsp. cornstarch

In a cast iron skillet, cook steaks. Add onions and salt to meat in skillet when seared. Let meat sweat twice before removing from pan. Set meat aside. In saucepan, cook cola, Worcestershire sauce, vinegar, basil, bouillon, garlic, and water over medium heat for 5 to 7 minutes. Mix cornstarch with water until it is slightly liquefied. Turn up the temperature to high. When sauce is boiling hard, add starch mixture slowly until sauce is soup-like in consistency. Turn down heat to medium; stir in liquid smoke and mushrooms. Cut meat into strips, add meat and onions to sauce, and remove from the heat. Let stand for 2 to 3 minutes before serving.

VENISON CASHEW STIR FRY

This dish has always been a favorite of mine. I love Asian food, and this dish is easy to prepare. There's no right or wrong item to add to stir-fry—add whatever you would like and have fun with it. The basic idea behind stir-fry is to cut all the vegetables and meats approximately the same size so they cook at the same rate. I recommend this for the vegetables, but I cook the venison first to preserve the flavor and tenderness. Stir-fry is usually served over rice, and if you can find it, jasmine rice is the finest Asian rice. It is aromatic, sweet, and holds together well, making it easier to eat with chopsticks.

1 lb. venison steaks

1 large onion

1 bunch fresh broccoli

2 cloves minced garlic

1 c. cashew halves

½ c. soy or teriyaki sauce

¼ c. oyster sauce

Optional Ingredients

¼ lb. snow peas

½ c. water chestnuts

1 red bell pepper

½ c. bean sprouts

½ c. small yellow squash, cut

Cut up all vegetables into equal-size pieces and place in a bowl. Cook meat in a cast iron skillet; use sesame oil if possible. Let meat sweat twice, adding salt to meat as desired. When meat is done, set aside. Stir fry vegetables, onions, and cashews in a large skillet or a wok until vegetables begin to brown slightly. Next add soy sauce and oyster sauce. Then stir in vegetables. Cut meat into similar-size chunks, add to stir-fry, and remove from heat. Serve over rice.

VENISON TIPS IN OYSTER SAUCE

This is a stir-fry spin-off with no vegetables. It is a quick, easy, and tasty dish when you want an oriental-style meal without the hassle. I recommend serving this over rice, but it goes equally well with steamed new potatoes.

1 lb. venison steaks

½ c. oyster sauce

¼ stick butter

1 tsp. hot sauce

Cook steaks in a cast iron skillet. When steak has sweated twice, remove from pan and set aside. Add butter and oyster sauce to pan and turn heat down to medium. Cut steak into strips, add to sauce, and remove from heat. Serve over rice or steamed new potatoes.

Venison with a Dijon Glaze

This is one of the few recipes that taste good cooked in a broiler. Easy to make, this venison tastes wonderful with fried potatoes and corn on the cob.

1 lb. venison steaks

½ lb. fresh bacon

6 Tbsp. Dijon mustard

3 Tbsp. honey

2 Tbsp. mayonnaise

1 Tbsp. vinegar

Wrap bacon around circumference of steaks. Preheat the broiler for 15 minutes to make sure it is plenty hot. Set steaks on broiler rack. Brush steaks with glaze made by mixing mustard, honey, mayonnaise, and vinegar. After 2 minutes, turn steaks over and glaze again. Then, 3 minutes later, pull steaks from broiler and let stand 3 minutes before serving.

TUSCAN VENISON

My inspiration for this recipe is the Tuscan region of Italy. Tuscany is known for growing very sweet onions. Choose sweet onions for this recipe to achieve the ultimate flavor. This meat is best served with wild rice and asparagus.

1 lb. venison steaks

1 large sweet onion

5 cloves garlic, sliced

4 Tbsp. sun-dried tomatoes, chopped

6 fresh basil leaves, chopped

1 fresh lemon, squeezed

2 sprigs fresh rosemary, chopped

6 Tbsp. brown sugar

6 Tbsp. Riesling wine or another sweet wine, such as a sherry

Create glaze by mixing all ingredients except onions and steak in a bowl. Cut onion directly in half from top to bottom, and separate the individual pieces. Preheat broiler for 15 minutes to make sure that it is hot. Place steaks on broiler rack, and add a large spoonful of glaze to each steak. Cover steaks with a full slice of onion. After 3 minutes, turn steak over and cover again with glaze and onion; 3 minutes later, remove steaks and let sit for 3 minutes before serving.

VENISON PEPPER MEDLEY

I made this recipe up one day because I was bored! I have no idea what influenced it. It is great served with a light summer meal; I like to eat it with chips and salsa, potato salad, and fresh fruit.

1 lb. venison steaks

1 red bell pepper

1 green bell pepper

1 orange or yellow bell pepper

1 Anaheim pepper

¼ c. beer

½ stick butter

Salt to taste

Cut peppers into bite-size pieces. Remove all veins and seeds. Cook peppers in a large skillet with butter until peppers begin to brown. In a separate skillet, cook steaks in a little oil, salting to taste once the meat is seared. When meat has sweated twice, pour beer and pepper over steaks and stir. Remove pan from heat and let stand for 2 to 3 minutes before serving.

Venison Summer Kabobs

This is another great summer recipe, ideal for an outdoor barbecue. Kabobs go well with summer salads, fresh fruit, and corn on the cob.

1 lb. venison steaks

1 lb. medium shrimp (raw)

1 sweet onion

2 large ruby red grapefruits

1 small zucchini or yellow squash

½ lb. button mushrooms (whole)

1 c. Italian dressing

2 large tomatoes

Begin by putting Italian dressing and steaks into a gallon-size plastic bag three hours before cooking. Agitate often. When you are ready to cook, cut everything except shrimp into one-inch pieces. Peel and devein shrimp. Place pieces on bamboo skewers. Preheat grill for 15 minutes to make sure it is plenty hot. Cook kabobs on the grill, turning only once until shrimp change colors totally and veggies are showing some char. When that happens, squeeze grapefruit liberally over kabobs. Remove from heat immediately and serve.

Kabobs are one of those dishes that everyone has tried at one time or another. What really makes these kabobs is the cooking process. Leaving kabobs on the grill too long always results in dry meat. Also, if the grill is not hot enough, the fats in the meat will be drawn out, leaving the meat tough. Feel free to add or change anything you want to the kabobs; these are simply suggested items.

Blackened Venison

This recipe stems from Cajun roots and varies greatly from recipe to recipe. One point is universal, however—the spices used need to char to give the food a blackened flavor. This recipe goes well with rice, fried okra, or collard greens.

1 lb. venison steaks

½ lb. bacon (precooked)

1 red bell pepper

1 tsp. coarse ground black pepper

½ tsp. cayenne pepper

1 tsp. molasses

1 small onion

2 cloves of garlic

¼ c. of crushed Ritz crackers or bread crumbs.

Precook bacon in a large skillet until crispy. Remove bacon and set aside. Do not discard grease. In a blender, blend bacon, pepper, red pepper, cayenne, molasses, onion, garlic, and Ritz crackers. Heat up the same pan with grease and add a little oil if needed. Cook steaks in pan. When you turn the meat the first time, spread blackened seasoning paste liberally on the seared part of steak. Do the same on the other side when you turn it over. Let meat sweat three times. Remove from pan. I usually like to set it on a plate lined with paper towels to drain a little of the oil from the blackened steak.

VENISON SWISS STEAKS

This is one of two recipes I've included that require that steaks cook for a long time at a low temperature. This recipe comes from Swiss origins, although I'm uncertain how directly the recipe ties into old-time recipes. This makes a great formal family dinner, such as a Sunday dinner. I like to serve it over boiled potato chunks.

2 lb. venison steaks

1 lb. breakfast sausage links

1 can crushed tomatoes

2 bay leaves

2 tsp. oregano

1 large onion

1 c. beer

5 Tbsp. honey

2 cubes chicken bouillon

Cut onions into rings, then caramelize in skillet, using sliver of butter. Remove from skillet and set aside. Cut sausage links into bite-size chunks and brown in a skillet. Remove from skillet and set aside. Lightly brown steaks in a skillet with hot oil on both sides and set aside. In a Crock-Pot or a Dutch oven, place all ingredients together and cook on low heat for three hours; serve. If you are using a Crock-Pot, set temperature to low setting. If you are using a Dutch oven, place it in your oven at 250 degrees, or use charcoals to establish that temperature. Watch this dish closely and add water if sauce becomes too low and starts to burn. When you are ready to serve this meal, sauce should be thick and soup-like in consistency.

BROWNED STEAKS OVER NEW POTATOES

This is the second of slow-cooked steak recipes. This also works well as a formal dinner served over new potatoes.

2 lb. venison steaks

½ lb. bacon, precooked

½ c. Worcestershire sauce

2 beef bouillon cubes

1 c. pearl onions, peeled

3 cloves garlic, sliced

2 bay leaves

5 Tbsp. liquid smoke

5 Tbsp. molasses

5 Tbsp. cider vinegar

1 c. water

Precook bacon in a skillet until crispy. Remove and set aside. When bacon has cooled, cut into small pieces. Heat skillet until bacon drippings start to smoke. Add steaks to pan and lightly brown meat on both sides. When meat is browned, remove from pan and discard the grease. In a Dutch oven or a Crock-Pot, add all remaining ingredients and cook at low temperature for three hours. When sauce is done, it should be gravy-like in consistency. Watch it closely to make sure there's enough liquid and meat doesn't burn. Serve over steamed new potatoes.

The author on a recent moose hunt in Alaska.

COOKING VENISON ROASTS

Venison roasts are ruined more often than any other cut of venison. The reason? Most people cook a venison roast as they would a beef roast. As I've said before, you wouldn't cook salmon as you would pork, so why cook venison as you would beef? Meats differ greatly, and methods of cooking should differ as well.

When you cook a venison roast, one method works well time and time again: cooking it slowly at a low temperature. This is the only way to ensure quality-tasting, tender venison every time. And the best way to cook venison slowly at a low temperature is in a Crock-Pot or Dutch oven. These two options provide you with a consistent, dependable cooking method. You can use your oven and a roasting pan, but you need to constantly watch it—and even so, the venison can end up dry and overcooked.

When you cook a venison roast, cook it at least three hours at two hundred degrees. If you cook it at any higher temperature, the proteins coagulate, causing the meat to be tough. If you don't cook it long enough, the internal temperature of the meat will not be high enough to kill off the bacteria.

If you cook a roast in a Crock-Pot, set the temperature on low. If you are using a Dutch oven, place it in your oven at two hundred degrees or follow the charcoal recommendations for two hundred degrees.

Another critical thing to note is that the liquid level in the pot or Dutch oven does not cover more than one third of the roast. This allows the roast to caramelize, giving you the great flavor you want in a roast. Even if the liquid level gets low, it should be fine as long as some liquid remains in the pan. However, too much liquid is truly detrimental. Meat will boil rather than caramelize when the liquid level is too high.

One other method remains to cook venison roasts, but it is tricky and produces varied results—especially for the novice. The fast-cook method works well for fillet-style roasts, such as loin roasts. You cook these types of roasts in a hot skillet or griddle at temperatures of 600 to 800 degrees. This sears the outside edges of the roast. Once the outside layer has been slightly charred, remove it from the pan or griddle and let it stand for a few minutes.

After the meat has been standing for about 5 minutes, split the roast in half down the middle. Heat up butter and a spice mix in your griddle or skillet, then place the meat, red side down, in the butter and cook for 5 minutes. This will produce some of the best-tasting roasts you will ever try. You'll find a few recipes for this type of cooking in this chapter.

When cooking venison roasts remember these tips:

- Cook the roasts at 200 degrees for at least three hours until meat pulls apart with a fork.

- Keep the liquid level at or below one third the roast.

- Use a Crock-Pot or a Dutch oven to cook your roasts, if possible; if not, cover your roasts with a lid or aluminium foil to retain moisture.

- Remove any excess fat or silver tissue before you cook you roast.

- Remove any damaged meat and let the meat sit in a little vinegar for 15 minutes before cooking.

PIONEER ROAST

Pioneer families would eat this roast cut from a deer that they would kill on their journey. It is a simple recipe but tastes great cooked in a Dutch oven. It goes well with Dutch-oven potatoes and any available fresh vegetables.

1 large venison roast, any type

1 large onion

1 apple (tart apples work the best)

1 Tbsp. brown sugar

¼ lb. bacon or 5 Tbsp. bacon grease

Water as needed to raise the level one third up the roast

Place roast in a Dutch oven and add all ingredients. Add water until roast is halfway covered. Cook roast for at least 3 hours at 200 degrees. Serve with potatoes. In pioneer time, this recipe would traditionally be put together midmorning, set in a metal bucket in the wagon, and covered by the coals of the morning cooking fire. The coals would provide just enough heat to slow cook the roast as they traveled. By the time they stopped for supper, the meat was tender and juicy. In our day, I cook the roast in my oven all day on a Sunday or in a pit while out hunting or camping.

Southwest Roast

This roast is a great roast for those who like southwest-style dishes. This recipe should be eaten with corn tortillas and beans.

1 venison roast

2 Anaheim peppers

1 large onion, sweet

4 cloves garlic, whole

1 packet of southwest marinade

1 lime, squeezed

1 jalapeno pepper

1 small can tomato sauce

Chop peppers and onion; set aside. In a Dutch oven or a Crock-Pot, add roast, seasoning packet, tomato sauce, garlic, and water until the mixture is one third up the roast. Cook for at least 3 hours at 200 degrees. Do not add any water unless the pan becomes dry; you want the liquid to thicken and caramelize. When roast is almost done, fry peppers and onions in a skillet with butter. When they are charred slightly, remove from heat and add to roast. Let the roast stand for 5 minutes, then serve.

BARBACOA

This is the traditional Mexican party dish which is served at weddings and birthdays. The traditional recipe is made from goat meat, but venison makes a fine substitute because of the similarities. Some of the ingredients have to be purchased in a Mexican food store.

1 large venison roast

1 large onion

4 cloves garlic

4 tsp. cumin

4 Tbsp. powdered anatole seed

2 Tbsp. Mexican oregano

2 Tbsp. New Mexico chiles, powdered

4 dried whole chile (arbol)

3 limes, squeezed

1 Tbsp. crushed black pepper

4 Tbsp. of vinegar

¼ c. fresh cilantro, chopped

2 small cans tomato sauce

Add all ingredients to a large Crock-Pot, Dutch oven, or a large saucepan. Add enough water to cover one third of roast. Do not add any more unless pan becomes dry. Cook for at least 3 hours on low heat. When meat is done, shred with a fork and allow all meat to be covered with sauce. Serve this meat in fresh corn tortillas with cooked pinto beans (not refried), fresh salsa, and guacamole. The recipe may seem a bit complicated, but it is well worth the effort.

WILD MOUNTAIN ROAST

This recipe has a woodsy flavor and is one of my signature dishes. It is fairly complicated to make but is very good. I like to serve it with a wild rice blend and asparagus.

1 large fillet-style venison roast (round roast works the best)

1 large onion, chopped

½ lb. breakfast sausage links, chopped

5 cloves garlic, sliced

1 lb. fresh spinach leaves

5 Tbsp. pine nuts, chopped (available in most grocery stores in the health food or produce aisles)

2 c. chopped cremini or portabello mushrooms

½ lb. bacon

3 c. port wine

1 c. broken bread pieces

2 eggs, whipped

Salt to taste

2 Tbsp. black pepper, crushed

¼ c. cream cheese

Begin by cutting roast along the grain, ½-inch thick, unrolling roast as you cut. When done, it should look like a flat, rectangular steak, such as a flank or skirt steak (these steaks can also be used in this recipe). Precook sausage links and chop into small, bite-size pieces. In a large bowl, add bread pieces, sausage, garlic, spinach leaves, pine nuts, and mushrooms. Stir together and add salt to taste. Whip eggs and cream cheese together until they begin to stiffen. Stir egg and cheese mixture into bread mixture.

Lay a sheet of waxed paper on a table. Lay three strips of basic natural twine across the wax paper. Lay bacon strips across twine in the opposite direction. Set rolled out roast on bacon. Add salt and pepper to roast. Add stuffing mixture to middle of roast, roll roast up, and tie together with twine. Set roast in a Dutch oven, and pour in wine and onions. Cook for at least 3 hours at 200 degrees. Serve by slicing roast into one-inch thick slices.

WINE-GLAZED VENISON

This roast is similar in flavor to the previous recipe, but it is much easier to make. Serve it with potatoes or rice and a green vegetable.

1 venison roast

1 large onion

4 cloves garlic, minced

1 Tbsp. rosemary

3 c. port wine

2 bay leaves

2 chicken bouillon cubes

Add all ingredients to a Crock-Pot or a Dutch oven. Cook for at least 3 hours at 200 degrees. Add water if pan becomes dry. Cut finished roast into slices and serve.

PULLED ROAST

This is a traditional Australian recipe that I have converted to venison. It is wonderful served with mashed potatoes and corn on the cob.

1 venison roast

1 onion, chopped

5 cloves garlic

3 cubes chicken bouillon

2 c. barbecue sauce

2 c. beer

1 bay leaf

Salt and pepper to taste

This is a very simple recipe. Throw all ingredients in a Dutch oven or a Crock-Pot, and let cook for at least 3 hours. When meat is done, pull apart with fork and make sure all meat is covered with sauce. Make enough to have leftovers because there is no better sandwich meat!

VENISON IN SALSA VERDE

This is a traditional Mexican recipe that I have converted to use for venison. It is very good made into tacos, enchiladas, or quesadillas. Serve it Mexican-style with beans, rice, and fresh salsa.

1 venison roast

3 c. verde salsa

1 fresh jalapeno, chopped

1 c. beer

Salt to taste

Add all ingredients to Dutch oven or Crock-Pot, and cook for at least 3 hours. Add water as needed to keep liquid level one third up the roast. When meat is done, pull apart with a fork, making sure meat is covered with sauce. Serve with fresh tortillas, beans, rice, and fresh salsa. This meat can be reused in different recipes, including quesadillas, tamales, and enchiladas.

VENISON IN SALSA ROJA

The only difference between this roast and the last is this is made with red salsa. It is tasty served with tortillas, beans, rice, and fresh salsa.

1 venison roast

3 c. medium red salsa

1 jalapeno, chopped

1 c. tomato sauce

½ c. beer

Add all ingredients to Dutch oven or Crock-Pot, and cook for at least 3 hours at 200 degrees. Add water as needed to keep liquid one third up roast. When done, pull apart with a fork and serve in tortillas. As with the previous recipe, this is versatile meat; I like to prepare several meals with it.

Swiss Roast

As the name implies, this recipe comes of Swiss origin, traditionally made in the late summer with fresh-grown mountain tomatoes and onions grown in the region. It is very good served with steamed potatoes or rice.

1 venison roast

2 large fresh tomatoes, diced

1 large onion, sliced

2 cloves garlic, minced

2 c. hoppy beer

1 bay leaf

4 Tbsp. vinegar

2 Tbsp. molasses

Salt to taste

Combine all ingredients in a Dutch oven or Crock-Pot and cook for at least 3 hours at 200 degrees. When done, cut across the grain in one-inch thick slices. Set the meat on a serving platter, and drizzle sauce over the top of the meat. Serve with potatoes or rice.

COCONUT CURRIED VENISON

This is a traditional India/Pakistan dish made with lamb. I have altered it for venison because of the meat similarities. It is best served over rice and with spinach or cabbage.

1 venison roast

1 8 oz. can coconut milk

5 Tbsp. mild curry powder

2 c. plain yogurt (sour cream can be substituted)

1 large onion

6 cloves garlic

2 sprigs fresh basil

1 8 oz. can crushed tomatoes

1 lemon, squeezed

4 Tbsp. liquid smoke

2 cubes chicken bouillon

Cut onion into slivers, and fry in butter until it begins to burn. Add curry powder to onion and cover with water. Add yogurt to onion and set aside. In a blender, puree tomatoes, basil, and garlic. Set roast, yogurt mix, and puree in a large Dutch oven or a Crock-Pot. Add liquid smoke and squeezed lemon. Cook for at least 3 hours, adding water as necessary to keep the liquid one third up roast. When roast is done, cut into chunks and serve over rice. Add salt to taste.

SLOPPY ROAST

This is a great roast for entertaining company. Easy to make, its mild flavor goes well with almost anything.

I venison roast

1 large onion

1 8 oz. can cream of mushroom soup

2 c. milk

1 c. mushrooms, chopped

1 c. sour cream

Salt to taste

Put ingredients into a Dutch oven or a Crock-Pot and cook for at least 3 hours at 200 degrees. When done, cut meat into one-inch thick slices. Serve with sauce over the top. This recipe goes well with potatoes or rice with corn.

ISLAND TERIYAKI ROAST

As the name implies, this recipe is influenced by Pacific Island flavors. This meat works wonderfully for an outside meal and is ideal served with lots of fresh fruit. It also tastes delicious served over rice.

1 venison roast

1 8 oz. can crushed pineapple

1 c. soy sauce

4 Tbsp. molasses

2 tsp. powdered ginger

2 Tbsp. brown sugar

Put all ingredients into a Dutch oven or Crock-Pot and cook at 200 degrees for at least 3 hours. When done, pull meat apart with a fork and make sure that all meat is covered with sauce.

CAJUN VENISON

This is traditional Cajun food from top to bottom. I like to eat this meat with cornbread and collard greens. It can be good served over rice or with potatoes added to the mix. Either way you do it, it packs quite a punch.

1 venison roast

¼ c. vegetable oil

¼ c. flour

1 large onion

1 c. tomato sauce

¼ c. Tabasco sauce

2 bay leaves

½ lb. bacon

1 8 oz. can black beans

2 cubes chicken bouillon

2 c. water

1 tsp. cayenne pepper

1 tsp. black pepper

4 Tbsp. vinegar

Start by making a roux, a staple of Cajun cooking. The roux takes about 30 minutes to make but is well worth it. To make the roux, heat oil in a skillet to medium heat. Gradually add flour, stirring constantly until mixture is chocolate brown. Add onions and meat, and brown them in roux. Immediately, add water and chicken bouillon. Put all ingredients in a Dutch oven or Crock-Pot, and cook for at least 3 hours at 200 degrees. When done, pull meat apart with a fork or cut it up into bite-size chunks, making sure that the meat is covered in sauce.

TRAIL BOSS ROAST

This is a recipe cooked on a chuckwagon on a cattle drive. I have altered it a bit to work for venison. It is one of my favorite camping roasts because it is good, hot, and full of energy for the day.

1 venison roast

3 8 oz. cans pinto beans

½ c. barbecue sauce

¼ c. Worcestershire sauce

5 Tbsp. honey

1 c. beer

Salt to taste

Add all ingredients in a Dutch oven or Crock-Pot, and cook for at least 3 hours at 200 degrees. When done, cut the meat into bite-size pieces and stir in beans. Serve with bread.

MESQUITE ROAST

This recipe is to be used with a loin or a center cut round roast and is excellent with almost any type of meal. It's my personal favorite venison roast recipe. This roast is unique in that it needs to be cooked hot and fast.

1 venison roast, center cut three to four inches in diameter

5 cloves garlic, sliced

1 packet mesquite marinade, dry

½ stick butter

6 Tbsp. Worcestershire sauce

Cut garlic cloves into slices. Place garlic into meat by inserting a thin knife blade into middle of roast and inserting the garlic slice. Next, heat oil in a skillet or a griddle until it begins to smoke. When oil smokes, set roast in oil and sear all the edges of meat. After meat has been seared, add mesquite marinade. Cook meat for about 10 minutes, turning over repeatedly. Remove roast from the pan, and let it sit for 5 minutes.

Heat butter and Worcestershire sauce in the same skillet or griddle. Split roast in half down the middle, and set it red side down in butter mix. Cook for 3 to 5 minutes, then remove from pan. Cut roast into 1-inch thick slices and serve.

Rosemary Roast

This recipe is cooked the same way as the previous recipe. The flavors in this roast hint of an Italian influence. This roast tastes wonderful with any type of potato or rice. It is best served with red bell peppers and dark green vegetables.

1 center cut loin or round venison roast

2 sprigs fresh rosemary

4 cloves garlic, minced

5 Tbsp. sun-dried tomatoes, chopped

1 lemon, squeezed

5 Tbsp. brown sugar

¼ c. Riesling wine

Salt to taste

To make a rub, mix all ingredients together and blend in a blender until pureed. Heat olive oil in a large skillet until it begins to smoke, then place roast in pan and sear all edges of roast. When roast has been seared, add rub liberally and cook for about 10 minutes. Next, split meat down the middle lengthwise and return to the skillet with the red portion down. Add a little extra wine to top of roast, and cook for 3 to 5 minutes. Cut into one-inch thick strips and serve.

JACK DANIELS ROAST

This recipe is not the sauce made famous by TGI Friday's. It is a great-tasting recipe of my own creation best served with twice-baked potatoes and yellow vegetables.

1 center cut venison roast such as a loin or a center round

½ c. Jack Daniels whiskey

¼ c. pineapple, crushed

2 Tbsp. black pepper, crushed

2 Tbsp. molasses

1 tsp. cloves, crushed

2 Tbsp. brown sugar

1 lemon, squeezed

Create rub by combining all ingredients together and blending into a puree. Heat oil in a skillet or a griddle until it begins to smoke. Add meat to skillet, and sear all edges of roast. Cook for 10 minutes. Add rub liberally to roast after it has been seared. When meat has cooked for 10 minutes, set aside for 5 minutes. Heat a little butter in the same skillet. Cut roast in half lengthwise, and set it in butter, red side down. Cook for 3 to 5 minutes, adding any remaining rub to roast. Cut roast into 1-inch thick slices and serve.

Ground Venison

Ground venison is my least favorite way to prepare venison because you lose much of the rich flavor that comes when cooking a roast or steak. It's impossible to preserve the delicate fats in ground meat when you cook it. In addition, most meat cutters add beef fat or suet to their venison when they grind it to help the meat stick together. The flavor of beef fat conflicts with the flavor of venison fat, and the result is never great. Pork fat is a much better substitute to blend in with venison. Finally, I am something of a gourmet cook, and ground meat doesn't often find its way into my style of cooking. However, I've included a couple of recipes in this section of the book that call for ground meat.

Ground venison can be used in a variety of everyday dishes. If you grind your own meat, I recommend not using any fat at all and using the meat for recipes that call for ground meat. If you want hamburgers, you are much better off buying beef patties; nothing you do will help venison stick together well. Because the ground meat loses the fats it has, it should not be cooked any differently than you would cook any other type of ground meat.

Easy Stroganoff

This is a family favorite! It is delicious served over egg noodles with corn. The prep time on this dish is only about 10 minutes, and the cost is minimal.

1 lb. ground venison

1 8 oz. can cream of mushroom soup

1 c. milk

1 c. sour cream

Brown the meat in a skillet. Add remaining ingredients and simmer for 5 to 7 minutes. Serve over egg noodles.

SWEDISH MEATBALLS

I learned this recipe from a Swedish friend of mine, and it's my favorite way to prepare ground venison. It is easy, and a lot of people love it. It is best served over rice or egg noodles.

1 lb. ground venison

½ lb. pork sausage, ground

1 c. bread crumbs

4 cloves garlic, minced

Salt to taste

1 8 oz. can cream of mushroom soup

1 c. sour cream

½ c. mushrooms, chopped

2 eggs, whipped

Begin by mixing venison, sausage, garlic, bread crumbs, and salt together. Whip eggs until they are twice their original volume. Stir eggs into meat. Form into meatballs. Set meatballs in a baking dish, and cover with mushroom soup, mushrooms, and sour cream. Bake at 400 degrees for 45 minutes. Let stand 5 minutes before serving.

About the Author

Matt Pelton grew up in Levan, Utah. This small community in central Utah is an ideal setting to pursue a passion for hunting. Matt was fascinated with wild game from the time he was a small child. He spent many hours watching his father butcher deer and elk, and Matt was always there to help cook. Determined to break out of the mold and find out all there is to know about cooking wild game, he has worked hard to hone his cooking skills during the past ten years.

Matt now resides in Provo, Utah, with his wife, Katie, and their children—Megan, five, and Tristan, three. When he isn't working, Matt can be found in the mountains hunting, fishing, or simply enjoying the outdoors. Matt's children have already developed a passion for hunting and the outdoors, watching hunting shows with their daddy and helping to prepare dinner almost every night.

0 26575 78685 9